Embedded Controllers
Using C and Arduino / 2E

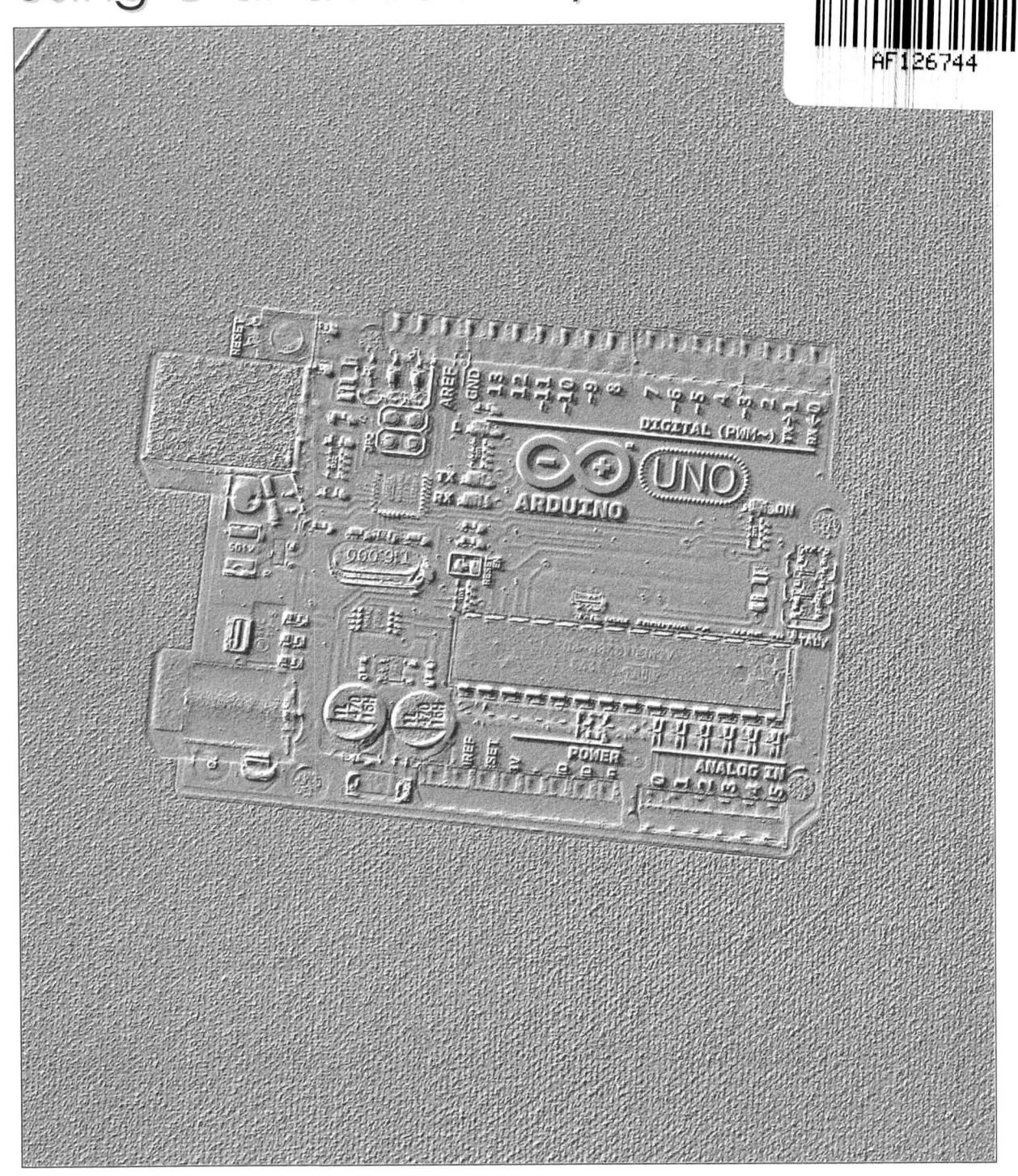

James M. Fiore

Embedded Controllers

Using C and Arduino

by

James M. Fiore

Version 2.1.9, 03 January 2021

This Embedded Controllers Using C and Arduino, by James M. Fiore is copyrighted under the terms of a Creative Commons license:

This work is freely redistributable for non-commercial use, share-alike with attribution

Published by James M. Fiore via dissidents

ISBN13: 978-1796854879

For more information or feedback, contact:

James Fiore, Professor
Electrical Engineering Technology
Mohawk Valley Community College
1101 Sherman Drive
Utica, NY 13501
jfiore@mvcc.edu

For the latest revisions, related titles, and links to low cost print versions, go to
www.mvcc.edu/jfiore or www.dissidents.com

YouTube Channel: *Electronics with Professor Fiore*

Cover art by the author

Introduction

This text is designed to introduce and expand upon material related to the C programming language and embedded controllers, and specifically, the Arduino development system and associated Atmel ATmega microcontrollers. It is intended to fit the time constraints of a typical 3 to 4 credit hour course for electrical engineering technology and computer engineering technology programs, although it could also fit the needs of a hardware-oriented course in computer science. As such, the text does not attempt to cover *every* aspect of the C language, the Arduino system or Atmel AVR microcontrollers. The first section deals with the C language itself. It is assumed that the student is a relative newcomer to the C language but has some experience with another high level language, for example, Python. This means concepts such as conditionals and iteration are already familiar and the student can get up and running fairly quickly. From there, the Arduino development environment is examined.

Unlike the myriad Arduino books now available, this text does not simply rely on the Arduino libraries. As convenient as the libraries may be, there are other, sometimes far more efficient, ways of programming the boards. Many of the chapters examine library source code to see "what's under the hood". This more generic approach means it will be easier for the student to use other processors and development systems instead of being tightly tied to one platform.

All Atmel schematics and data tables are derived from the latest version (2016) of the Atmel 328P documentation which may be found at http://www.atmel.com/devices/ATMEGA328P.aspx This serves as the final word on the operation and performance of the 328P and all interested parties should become familiar with it.

There is a companion laboratory manual to accompany this text. Other OER (Open Educational Resource) laboratory manuals in this series include Computer Programming with Python, and Science of Sound. OER texts and laboratory manuals are available for Operational Amplifiers & Linear Integrated Circuits, Semiconductor Devices, DC Electrical Circuit Analysis and AC Electrical Circuit Analysis. Please check my web sites for the latest versions.

A Note from the Author

This text is used at Mohawk Valley Community College in Utica, NY, for our ABET accredited AAS program in Electrical Engineering Technology. Specifically, it is used in our second year embedded controllers course. I am indebted to my students, co-workers and the MVCC family for their support and encouragement of this project. While it would have been possible to seek a traditional publisher for this work, as a long-time supporter and contributor to freeware and shareware computer software, I have decided instead to release this using a Creative Commons non-commercial, share-alike license. I encourage others to make use of this manual for their own work and to build upon it. If you do add to this effort, I would appreciate a notification.

> *"When things get so big, I don't trust them at all*
> *You want some control-you gotta keep it small"*
>
> *- Peter Gabriel*

Table of Contents

1. Course Introduction 8
2. C Memory Organization 10
3. C Language Basics 14
4. C Language Basics II 24
5. C Storage Types and Scope 32
6. C Arrays and Strings 36
7. C Conditionals and Looping 40
8. C Pointers and Addresses 48
9. C Look-Up Tables 52
10. C Structures 56
11. C Linked Lists* 60
12. C Memory* 64
13. C File I/O* 68
14. C Command Line Arguments* . . . 72
15. Embedded Programming 74
16. Hardware Architecture 78
17. AVR ATmega 328P Overview** . . . 84
18. Bits & Pieces: includes and defines . . 90
19. Bits & Pieces: Digital Output Circuitry . . 98
20. Bits & Pieces: Digital Input Circuitry . . 102
21. Bits & Pieces: pinMode 106
22. Bits & Pieces: digitalWrite . . . 112
23. Bits & Pieces: delay 116
24. Bits & Pieces: digitalRead . . . 124
25. Bits & Pieces: Analog Input Circuitry . . 132
26. Bits & Pieces: analogRead . . . 136
27. Bits & Pieces: analogWrite . . . 142
28. Bits & Pieces: Timer/Counters . . . 146
29. Bits & Pieces: Interrupts . . . 154

Appendices 160

Index 165

* Included for language coverage but seldom used for small to medium scale embedded work.
** Including modest comic relief for *film noir* buffs.

Embedded Controllers

1. Course Introduction

1.1 Overview

This course introduces the C programming language and specifically addresses the issue of embedded programming. It is assumed that you have worked with some other high level language before, such as Python, BASIC, FORTRAN or Pascal. Due to the complexities of embedded systems, we begin with a typical desktop system and examine the structure of the language along with basic examples. Once we have a decent grounding in syntax, structure, and the development cycle, we switch over to an embedded system, namely an Arduino based development system.

This course is designed so that you can do considerable work at home with minimal cost if you choose to (this is entirely optional, but programming these little beasties can be addicting so be forewarned). Along with this course text and the associated lab manual, you will need an Arduino Uno board (about $25) and a USB host cable. A small "wall wart" power adapter for it may also be useful. There's a lot of free C programming info on the Internet but if you prefer print books and want more detail, you may also wish to purchase one of the many C programming texts available. Two good titles are Kochan's book *Programming in C* and the one by Deitel & Deitel, *C-How to Program*. Whichever book you choose, make sure that its focus is C and not C++. You will also need a desktop C compiler. Just about any will do, including Visual C/C++, Borland, CodeWarrior, or even GCC. A couple of decent freeware compilers available on the Internet include Pelles C and Miracle C.

1.2 Frequently Asked Questions

Why learn C language programming?

C is perhaps the most widely used development language today. That alone is a good reason to consider it but there's more:

- It is a modern structured language that has been standardized (ANSI).
- It is modular, allowing reuse of code.
- It is widely supported, allowing source code to be used for several different platforms by just recompiling for the new target.
- Its popularity means that several third-party add-ons (libraries and modules) are available to "stretch" the language.
- It has type checking which helps catch errors.
- It is very powerful, allowing you to get "close to the metal".
- Generally, it creates very efficient code (small space and fast execution).

What's the difference between C and C++?

C++ is a superset of C. First came C, then came C++. In fact, the name C++ is a programmer's joke because ++ is the increment operator in C. Thus, C++ literally means "increment C", or perhaps "give me the next C". C++ does everything C does plus a whole lot more. These extra features don't come free and embedded applications usually cannot afford the overhead. Consequently, although much desktop work is done in C++ as well as C, most embedded work is done in C. Desktop development systems are usually referred to as C/C++ systems meaning that they'll do both. Embedded development systems may be strictly C or even a variant of it (as is ours).

Where can I buy an Arduino development board?

The Arduino Uno board is available from a variety of sources including Digi-Key, Mouser, Parts Express and others. Shop around!

What's the difference between desktop PC development and embedded programming?

Desktop development focuses on applications for desktop computers. These include things like word processors, graphing utilities, games, CAD programs, etc. These are the things most people think of when they hear the word "computer". Embedded programming focuses on the myriad nearly invisible applications that surround us every day. Examples include the code that runs your microwave oven, automobile engine management system, cell phone, and many others. In terms of total units, embedded applications far outnumber desktop applications. You may have one or even a few PCs in your house but you probably use dozens of embedded applications every day. Embedded microcontrollers tend to be much less powerful but also much less expensive than their PC counterparts. The differing programming techniques are an integral part of this course and we shall spend considerable time examining them.

How does C compare with Python?

If, like many students taking this course, your background is with the Python language, you may find certain aspects of C a little odd at first. Some of it may seem overly complicated. Do not be alarmed though. The core of the language is actually simple. Python tends to hide things from the programmer while C doesn't. Initially, this seems to make things more complicated, and it does for the most simple of programs, but for more complicated tasks C tends to cut to the heart of the matter. Many kinds of data and hardware manipulation are much more direct and efficient in C than in other languages. One practical consideration is that C is a compiled language while most versions of Python are essentially interpreted. This means that there is an extra step in the development cycle, but the resulting compiled program is much more efficient. We will examine why this is so a little later.

How does C compare with assembly language?

Assembly has traditionally been used when code space and speed are of utmost importance. Years ago, virtually all embedded work was done in assembly. As microcontrollers have increased in power and the C compilers have improved, the tables have turned. The downside of assembly now weighs against it. Assembly is processor-specific, unstructured, not standardized, nor particularly easy to read or write. C now offers similar performance characteristics to assembly but with all the advantages of a modern structured language.

2. C Memory Organization

2.1 Introduction

When programming in C, it helps if you know at least a little about the internal workings of simple computer systems. As C tends to be "close to the metal", the way in which certain things are performed as well preferred coding techniques will be more apparent.

First off, let's narrow the field a bit by declaring that we will only investigate a fairly simple system, the sort of thing one might see in an embedded application. That means a basic processor and solid state memory. We won't worry about disk drives, monitors, and so forth. Specific details concerning controller architecture, memory hardware and internal IO circuitry are covered in later chapters.

2.2 Guts 101

A basic system consists of a control device called a CPU (central processing unit), microprocessor, or microcontroller. There are subtle distinctions between these but we have little need to go very deep at this point. Microcontrollers tend not to be as powerful as standard microprocessors in terms of processing speed but they usually have an array of input/output ports and hardware functions (such as analog-to-digital or digital-to-analog converters) on chip that typical microprocessors do not. To keep things simple we shall use the term "processor" as a generic.

Microprocessors normally are connected to external memory (RAM chips). Microcontrollers generally contain sufficient on-board memory to alleviate this requirement but it is worthwhile to note that we are not talking about large (megabyte) quantities. A microcontroller may only contain a few hundred bytes of memory but in simple applications that may be sufficient. Remember, a byte of memory consists of 8 bits, each bit being thought of as a 1/0, high/low, yes/no, or true/false pair.

In order for a processor to operate on data held in memory, the data must first be copied into a processor's register (it may have dozens of registers). Only in a register can mathematical or logical operations be carried out. For example, if you desire to add one to a variable, the value of the variable must first be copied into a register. The addition is performed on the register contents yielding the answer. This answer is then copied back to the original memory location of the variable. It seems a little roundabout at first, but don't worry, the C language compiler will take care of most of those details for you.

2.3 Memory Maps

Every byte of memory in a computer system has an address associated with it. This is a requirement. Without an address, the processor has no way of identifying a specific location in memory. Generally, memory addressing starts at 0 and works its way up, although some addresses may be special or "reserved" in some systems. That is, a specific address might not refer to normal memory, but instead might refer to a certain input/output port for external communication. Very often it is useful to draw a *memory map*. This is nothing more than a huge array of memory slots. Some people draw them with the lowest (starting) address at the top and other people draw them with the lowest address at the bottom.

Here's an example with just six bytes of memory:

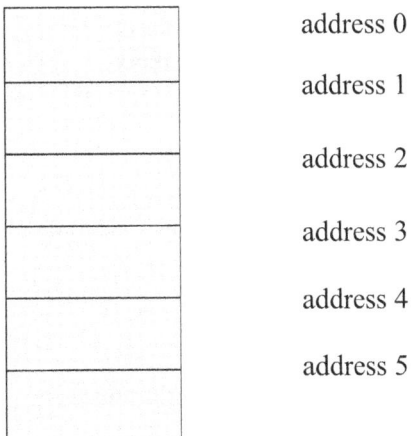

Figure 2.1, simple memory map

Each address or slot represents a place we can store one byte. If we had to remember specific addresses we would be doing a lot of work. Instead, the C compiler will keep track of this for us. For example, if we declare a `char` named X, it might be at address 2. If we need to print that value, we don't have to say "fetch the value at address 2". Instead we say; "fetch the value of X" and the compiler generates code to make this work out to the proper address (2). This abstraction eases our mental burden considerably. As many variables require more than one byte, we may need to combine addresses to store a single value. For example, if we chose a `short int`, that needs two bytes. Suppose this variable starts at address 4. It will also require the use of address 5. When we access this variable the compiler automatically generates the code to utilize both addresses because it "knows" we're using a `short int`. Our little six byte memory map could hold 6 `char`, 3 `short int`, 1 `long int` with 1 `short int`, 1 `long int` with 2 `char`, or some other similar combination. It cannot hold a `double` as that requires 8 bytes. Similarly, it could not hold an array of 4 or more `short int` (see Chapter Three for details on numeric data types).

Arrays are of special interest as they must be contiguous in memory. For example, suppose a system has 1000 bytes of memory and a 200 element char array was declared. If this array starts at address 500 then all of the slots from 500 through 699 are allocated for the array. It cannot be created in "scattered" fashion with a few bytes here and a few bytes there. This requirement is due to the manner in which arrays are indexed (accessed), as we shall see later.

2.4 Stacks

Many programs need only temporary storage for certain variables. That is, a variable may only be used for a limited time and then "thrown away". It would be inefficient to allocate permanent space for this sort of variable. In its place, many systems use a *stack*. Ordinarily, an application is split into two parts, a code section and a data section. The data section contains the "permanent" (global) data. As these two will not consume the entire memory map, the remainder of the memory is often used for temporary storage via a stack. The stack starts at the opposite end of the memory map and grows toward the code and data sections. It is called a First-In-Last-Out stack or FILO stack. It works like a stack of trays in a cafeteria. The first tray placed on the stack will be the last one pulled off and vice versa. When temporary variables are needed, this memory area is used. As more items are needed, more memory is taken up. As our code exits from a function, the temporary (`auto`) variables declared there are no longer needed, and the stack shrinks. If we make many, many function calls with many, many declared variables, it is possible for the stack to overrun the code and data sections of our program. The system is now corrupt, and proper execution and functioning of the program are unlikely.

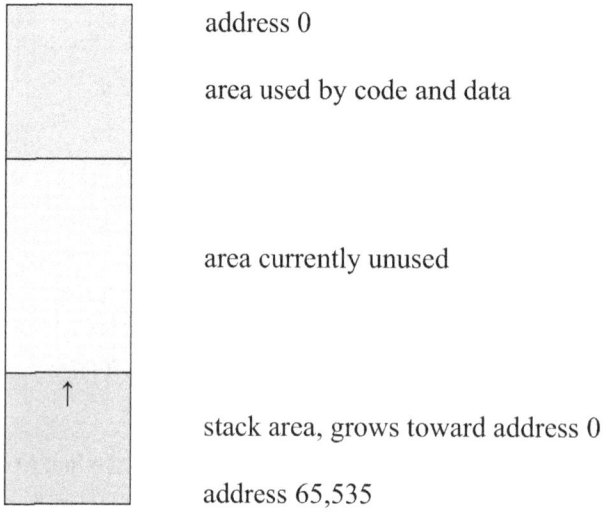

address 0

area used by code and data

area currently unused

stack area, grows toward address 0

address 65,535

Figure 2.2, basic memory layout

Above is a memory map example of a system with 64k bytes of memory (k=1024 or 2^{10}). Individual memory slots are not shown. Only the general areas are shown.

It is worthwhile to note that in some systems, code and data are in a common area as shown (Von Neumann architecture) while in others they are physically split (Harvard architecture). Whether split or not, the basic concepts remain. So, why would we want to split the two areas, each accessed via its own memory bus[1]? Simple, separating the code and data allows the processor to fetch the next instruction (code) using a memory bus that is physically separate from the data bus it is currently accessing. A shared code/data memory bus would require special timing to coordinate this process as only one thing can be on the bus at any given time. Having two separate memory buses will speed execution times.

---

[1] A *bus* typically refers to a collection of wires or connections upon which multiple data bits (or address bits) are sent as a group.

3. C Language Basics

3.1 Introduction

C is a terse language. It is designed for professional programmers who need to do a lot with a little code quickly. Unlike BASIC or Python, C is a compiled language. This means that once you have written a program, it needs to be fed into a compiler that turns your C language instructions into machine code that the microprocessor or microcontroller can execute. This is an extra step, but it results in a more efficient program than an interpreter. An interpreter turns your code into machine language while it's running, essentially a line at a time. This results in slower execution. Also, in order to run your program on another machine, that machine must also have an interpreter on it. You can think of a compiler as doing the translation all at once instead of a line at a time.

Unlike many languages, C is not line oriented, but is instead free-flow. A program can be thought of as consisting of three major components: Variables, statements and functions. Variables are just places to hold things, as they are in any other language. They might be integers, floating point (real) numbers, or some other type. Statements include things such as variable operations and assignments (i.e., set x to 5 times y), tests (i.e., is x more than 10?), and so forth. Functions contain statements and may also call other functions.

3.2 Variable Naming, Types and Declaration

Variable naming is fairly simple. Variable names are a combination of letters, numerals, and the underscore. Upper and lower case can be mixed and the length is typically 31 characters max, but the actual limit depends on the C compiler in use. Further, the variable name cannot be a reserved (key) word nor can it contain special characters such as . ; , * - and so on. So, legal names include things like `x`, `volts`, `resistor7`, or even `I_Wanna_Go_Home_Now`.

C supports a handful of variable types. These include floating point or real numbers in two basic flavors: `float`, which is a 32 bit number, and `double`, which is a higher precision version using 64 bits. There are also a few integer types including `char`, which is 8 bits, `short int`, which is 16 bits, and `long int`, which is 32 bits. As `char` is 8 bits, it can hold 2 to the 8th combinations, or 256 different values. This is sufficient for a single ASCII character, hence the name. Similarly, a `short int` (or `short`, for short!) can hold 2 to the 16th combinations, or 65,536 values. `char`s and `int`s may be `signed` or `unsigned` (`signed`, allowing negative values, is the default). There is also a plain old `int`, which might be either 16 or 32 bits, depending on which is most efficient for the compiler (to be on the safe side, never use plain old `int` if the value might require more than 16 bits).

Sometimes you might also come across special double long integers (also called long longs) that take up 8 bytes as well as 80 bit extended precision floats (as defined by the IEEE).

Here is a table to summarize the sizes and ranges of variables:

Variable Type	Bytes Used	Minimum	Maximum
char	1	−128	127
unsigned char	1	0	255
short int	2	−32768	32767
unsigned short int	2	0	65535
long int	4	≈ −2 billion	≈ 2 billion
unsigned long int	4	0	≈ 4 billion
float (6 significant digits)	4	$\pm 1.2 \text{ E} -38$	$\pm 3.4 \text{ E} +38$
double (15 significant digits)	8	$\pm 2.3 \text{ E} -308$	$\pm 1.7 \text{ E} +308$

Figure 3.1, numeric types and ranges

C also supports arrays and compound data types. We shall examine these in a later segment.

Variables must be declared before they are used. They cannot be created on a whim, so to speak, as they are in Python. A declaration consists of the variable type followed by the variable name, and optionally, an initial value. Multiple declarations are allowed. Here are some examples:

```
char x;              declares a signed 8 bit integer called x
unsigned char y;     declares an unsigned 8 bit integer called y
short z, a;          declares two signed 16 bit integers named z and a
float b =1.0;        declares a real number named b and sets its initial value to 1.0
```

Note that each of these declarations is followed with a semi-colon. The semi-colon is the C language way of saying "This statement ends here". This means that you can be a little sloppy (or unique) in your way of dealing with spaces. The following are all equivalent and legal:

```
float b = 1.0;
float b=1.0;
float    b  =   1.0 ;
```

3.3 Functions

Functions use the same naming rules as variables. All functions use the same template that looks something like this:

```
return_value function_name( function argument list )
{
    statement(s)
}
```

Figure 3.1, basic function template

You might think of the function in the mathematical sense. That is, you give it some value(s) and it gives you back a value. For example, your calculator has a sine function. You send it an angle and it gives you back a value. In C, functions may have several arguments, not just one. They might not even have an argument. Also, C functions may return a value, but they don't have to. The "guts" of the function are defined within the opening and closing brace pair { }. So, a function which takes two integers, x and y, as arguments, and returns a floating point value will look something like this:

```
float my_function( int x, int y )
{
    //...appropriate statements here...
}
```

If the function doesn't take or return values, the word `void` is used. If a function neither requires values nor returns a value, it would look like:

```
void other_function( void )
{
    //...appropriate statements here...
}
```

This may appear to be extra fussy work at first, but the listing of data types makes a lot of sense because C has something called *type checking*. This means that if you try to send a function the wrong kind of variable, or even the wrong number of variables, the compiler will warn you that you've made a mistake! Thus if you try to send `my_function()` above two floats or three integers, the compiler will complain and save you a big headache during testing.

All programs must have a place to start, and in C, program execution begins with a function called `main`. This does not have to be the first function written or listed, but all programs must have a function called `main`. Here's our first program, found in Figure 3.2, following:

```
/* Our first program */

void main( void )
{
        float x = 2.0;
        float y = 3.0;
        float z;

        z = x*y/(x+y);
}
```

Figure 3.2, a simple program

There is only one function here, `main()`. It takes no variables and returns nothing. What's the other stuff? First, the `/* */` pair denotes a comment[2]. Anything inside of the comment pair is ignored by the compiler. A C comment can stretch for many lines. Once inside the function, three variables are declared with two of them given initial values. Next, the variables `x` and `y` are multiplied together, divided by their sum, and assigned to `z`. As C is free-flow, an equivalent (but ugly) version is:

```
/* Our first program */ void main(void){
float x=2.0;float y=3.0;float z;z=x*y/(x+y);}
```

Figure 3.3, alternate format (to be avoided)

This is the complete opposite of Python which has very rigid spacing and formatting rules.

Now, suppose that this add, multiply, divide operation is something that you need to do a lot. We could split this off into a separate function. Our program now looks like Figure 3.4 on the following page:

---

[2] C also allows // to denote a single line comment without the "backend pairing".

Embedded Controllers

```
/* Our second program */

float add_mult_div( float a,  float b )
{
        float answer;

        answer = a*b/(a+b);
        return( answer );
}

void main( void )
{
        float x = 2.0;
        float y = 3.0;
        float z;

        z = add_mult_div( x, y );
}
```

Figure 3.4, program with separate function

The new math function takes two `float`s as arguments and returns a `float` to the caller. The compiler sees the new function before it is used in `main()`, thus, it already "knows" that it should be sent two `float`s and that the return value must be assigned to a `float`. It is very important to note that the new math function uses different variable names (`a` and `b`) from the caller (`x` and `y`). The variables in the new math function are really just place-holders. The values from the original call (`x` and `y`) are copied to these new variables (`a` and `b`) and used within the new function. As they are copies, they can be altered without changing the original values of `x` and `y`. In this case, `x` and `y` are said to be *local* to the `main()` function while `a` and `b` are *local* to the `add_mult_div()` function. In other words, `a` isn't visible from `main()` so you can't accidentally alter it! Similarly, `x` isn't visible from `add_mult_div()`, so you can't accidentally alter it either. This is a positive boon when dealing with large programs using many variable names. While it's not usually preferred, there are times when you want a variable to be known "everywhere". These are called *global* items. You can make variables *global* by simply declaring them at the beginning of the program outside of the functions (i.e., right after that initial comment in our example).

3.4 Libraries

The examples above are rather limited because, although they perform a calculation, we have no way of seeing the result! We need some way to print the answer to the computer screen. To do this, we rely on system functions and libraries. There are a series of libraries included with most C development systems to cover a variety of needs. Essentially, someone has already coded, tested and compiled a bunch of functions for you. You add these functions to your program through a process called *linking*. Linking simply combines your compiled code along with any required library code into a final executable program. For basic printouts, data input, and the like, we use the *standard IO (Input/Output) library*, or *stdio* for short. There is a function in this library named `printf()` for "print formatted". So that the compiler can do type checking, it must know something about this new function. We tell the compiler to look into a special file called a *header file* to find this information. Every library will have an associated header file (usually of the same name) and it will normally end with a .h file extension[3]. The compiler directive is called an `include` statement.

```c
// Our third program, this is an example of a single line comment

#include <stdio.h>

void main( void )
{
        printf("Hello world.\n");
}
```

Figure 3.5, program with library function call

This program simply prints the message *Hello world.* to the screen. The backslash-n combo is a special formatting token that means *add a new line* (i.e., bring the cursor to the line below). If we did not add the `#include` directive, the compiler wouldn't know anything about `printf()`, and would complain when we tried to use it. So, what's in a header file? Well, among other things they contain *function prototypes*. The prototypes are nothing more than a template. You can create your own by cutting and pasting your function name with argument list and adding a semicolon to it. Here is the function prototype for our earlier math function:

```c
float add_mult_div( float a, float b );
```

You could make your own library of functions if you want. To use them, all you'd need is an appropriate `include` statement in your code, and remember to add in your library code with the linker. This will allow you to reuse code and save time. We will look at multiple file projects and more on libraries in a later segment.

Consequently, if we want to print out the answer to the first program, we'd wind up with something like Figure 3.6 on the following page:

---

[3] It is worth noting that a large number of subgroups of code are collected together into what is referred to as the *C standard library*. The precise implementation of this is dependent on the operating system, however, the header files (e.g., stdio.h, string.h, math.h, etc.) remain distinct.

Embedded Controllers

```
/* Our fourth program */

#include <stdio.h>

void main( void )
{
        float x = 2.0;
        float y = 3.0;
        float z;

        z = x*y/(x+y);

        printf("The answer is %f\n", z);
}
```

Figure 3.6, a more complete program

The `%f` in the `printf()` function serves as a place holder for the variable `z`. If you need to print several values you can do something like this:

```
printf("The answer from %f and %f is %f\n", x, y, z);
```

In this case, the first `%f` is used for x, the second `%f` for y, and the final one for z. The result will look like:

```
The answer from 2.0 and 3.0 is 1.2
```

3.5 Some Simple Math

C uses the same basic math operators as many other languages. These include +, −, /(divide), and *(multiply). Parentheses are used to group elements and force hierarchy of operations. C also includes `%` for modulo. Modulo is an integer operation that leaves the remainder of a division, thus 5 modulo 7 is 2.

The divide behaves a little differently with integers than with floats as there can be no remainder. Thus 9 integer divide 4 is 2, not 2.25 as it would be if you were using floats. C also has a series of bit manipulators that we will look at a little later. For higher math operations, you will want to look at the math library (`math.h` header file). Some examples are `sin()`, `cos()`, `tan()`, `log10()` (common log) and `pow()` for powers and roots. Do **not** try to use ^ as you do on many calculators. x raised to the y power is **not** x^y but rather `pow(x, y)`. The ^ operator has an entirely different meaning in C! Recalling what we said earlier about libraries, if you wanted to use a function like `sin()` in your code, you'd have to tell the compiler where to find the prototype and similar info. At the top of your program you'd add the line:

```
#include <math.h>
```

A final caution: The examples above are meant to be clear, but not necessarily the most efficient way of doing things. As we shall see, sometimes the way you code something can have a huge impact on its performance. Given the power of C, expert programmers can sometimes create code that is nearly indecipherable for ordinary people. There is a method behind the apparent madness.

3.6 The program creation/development cycle

To create a C program:

1. Do the requisite mental work. This is the most important part.
2. Create the C source code. This can be done using a text editor, but is normally done within the IDE (Integrated Development Environment). C source files are plain text and saved with a ".c" extension.
3. Compile the source code. This creates an assembly output file. Normally, compiling automatically fires up the assembler, which turns the assembly file into a machine language output file.
4. Link the output file with any required libraries using the linker. This creates an executable file. For desktop development, this is ready to test.
5. For embedded development, download the resulting executable to the target hardware (in our case, the Arduino development board). For the Arduino, steps 3, 4, and 5 can be combined by selecting "Build" from the IDE menu.
6. Test the executable. If it doesn't behave properly, go back to step one.

3.7 Summary

Here are some things to keep in the back of your mind when learning C:

- C is terse. You can do a lot with a little code.
- As it allows you to do almost anything, a novice can get into trouble very quickly.
- It is a relatively thin language, meaning that most "system functions" are not part of the language per se, but come from link-time libraries.
- Function calls, function calls, and more function calls!
- Source code is free flow, not line oriented. A "line" of code is usually terminated with a semicolon.
- Shortcuts allow experts to create code that is almost indecipherable by normal programmers.
- All variables must be declared before use (not free flow as in Python).
- Variables can be global or local in scope. That is, a local variable can be "known" in one place of the program and not in another.

3.8 Exercises

1. Write a C code comment that includes your name and the date. Use both the single line and the multi-line styles.

2. Write a function that will take three floating point values as arguments. The function should return the average value of the three arguments.

3. Write a program that will print out your name.

4. C Basics II

4.1 Input and Output

We've seen the use of `printf()` to send information to the computer screen. `printf()` is a very large and complicated function with many possible variants of format specifiers. Format specifiers are the "% things" used as placeholders for values. Some examples are:

```
%f    float
%lf   double (long float)
%e    float using exponent notation
%g    float using shorter of e or f style
%d    decimal integer
%ld   decimal long integer
%x    hexadecimal (hex or base 16) integer
%o    octal (base 8) integer
%u    unsigned integer
%c    single character
%s    character string
```

Figure 4.1, print format types

Suppose that you wanted to print out the value of the variable ans in decimal, hex, and octal. The following instruction would do it all:

```
printf("The answer is %d, or hex %x, or octal %o.\n", ans, ans, ans );
```

Note how the three variables are labeled. This is important. If you printed something in hex without some form of label, you might not know if it was hex or decimal. For example, if you just saw the number "23", how would you know it's 23 decimal or 23 hex (35 decimal)? For that matter, how would you set a hex constant in your C code? The compiler would have no way of "knowing" either. To get around this, hex values are prefixed with 0x. Thus, we have 0x23 for hex 23. The `printf()` function does not automatically add the 0x on output. The reason is because it may prove distracting if you have a table filled only with hex values. It's easy enough to use 0x%d instead of just %d for the output format.

You can also add a field width specifier. For example, %5d means print the integer in decimal with 5 spaces minimum. Similarly, %6.2f means print the floating point value using 6 spaces minimum. The ".2" portion is a precision specifier and in this case indicates 2 digits after the decimal point are to be used. As you can see, this is a very powerful and flexible function!

The mirror input function is `scanf()`. This is similar to Python's input statement. Although you can ask for several values at once, it is generally best to ask for a single value when using this function. It uses the same sort of format specifiers as `printf()`. There is one important point to note. The `scanf()` function needs to know where to place the entered value in computer memory. Simply informing it of the name of the variable is insufficient. You must tell it where in memory the variable is, in other words, you must specify the address of the variable. C uses the `&` operator to signify "address of". For example, if you wish to obtain an integer from the user and place it in a variable called `voltage`, you might see a program fragment like so...

```
printf("Please enter the voltage:");
scanf("%d", &voltage);
```

It is very common for new programmers to forget the &. Be forewarned!

4.2 Variable Sizes

A common question among new programers is "Why are there so many sizes of variables available?" We have two different sizes of reals; `float` at 32 bits, and `double` at 64 bits. We also have three different sizes of intgers at 8, 16, and 32 bits each[4]. In many languages, there's just real and integer with no size variation, so why does C offer so many choices? The reason is that "one size **doesn't** fit all". You have options in order to optimize your code. If you have a variable that ranges from say, 0 to 1000, there's no need to use more than a short (16 bit) integer. Using a 32 bit integer simply uses more memory. Now, you might consider 2 extra bytes to be no big deal, but remember that we are talking about embedded controllers in some cases, not desktop systems. Some small controllers may have only a few hundred bytes of memory available for data. Even on desktop systems with gigabytes of memory, choosing the wrong size can be disastrous. For example, suppose you have a system with an analog to digital converter for audio. The CD standard sampling rate is 44,100 samples per second. Each sample is a 16 bit value (2 bytes), producing a data rate of 88,100 bytes per second. Now imagine that you need enough memory for a five minute song in stereo. That works out to nearly 53 megabytes of memory. If you had chosen long (32 bit) integers to hold these data, you'd need about 106 megabytes instead. As the values placed on an audio CD never exceed 16 bits, it would be foolish to allocate more than 16 bits each for the values. Data sizes are power-of-2 multiples of a byte though, so you can't choose to have an integer of say, 22 bits length. It's 8, 16, or 32 for the most part (some controllers have an upper limit of 16 bits).

In the case of `float` versus `double`, `float` is used where space is at a premium. It has a smaller range (size of exponent) and a lower precision (number of significant digits) than `double`. `double` is generally preferred and is the norm for most math functions. Plain floats are sometimes referred to as *singles* (that is, single precision versus double precision).

If you don't know the size of a particular data item (for example an `int` might be either 16 or 32 bits depending on the hardware and compiler), you can use the `sizeof()` command. This looks like a function but it's really built into the language. The argument is the item or expression you're interested in. It returns the size required in bytes.

```
size = sizeof( int );
```

`size` will be either 2 or 4 depending on the system.

---

[4] In some systems 80 bit doubles and/or 64 bit integers are also available.

4.3 More Math

OK, so what happens if you add or multiply two `short int` together and the result is more than 16 bits long? You wind up with an overrange condition. Note that the compiler cannot warn you of this because whether or not this happens will depend entirely on values entered by the user and subsequently computed within the program. Hopefully, you will always consider maximum value cases and choose appropriate data sizes and this won't be a problem. But what actually happens? To put it simply, the top most bits will be ignored. Consider an 8 bit unsigned integer. It goes from 0 to 255. 255 is represented as eight 1s. What happens if you add the value 1 to this? You get a 9 bit number: a 1 followed by eight 0s. That ninth bit is thrown away as the variable only has eight bits. Thus, 255 plus 1 equals 0! This can create some serious problems! For example, suppose you wanted to use this variable as a loop counter. You want to go through a loop 500 times. The loop will never terminate because an 8 bit integer can't go up that high. You keep adding one to it, but it keeps flipping back to 0 after it hits 255. This behavior is not all bad; it can, in fact, be put to good use with things like interrupts and timers, as we shall see.

What happens if you mix different types of variables? For example, what happens if you divide a `double` by an `int` or a `float` by `double`? C will *promote* the lesser size/precision types to the larger type and then do the operation. This can sometimes present a problem if you try to assign the result back to something smaller, even if you know it will always "fit". The compiler will complain if you divide a `long int` by another `long int` and try to assign the result to a `short int`. You can get around this by using a *cast*. This is your way of telling the compiler that you know there is a potential problem, but to go ahead anyway (hopefully, because you know it will always work, not just because you want to defeat the compiler warning). Casting in C is similar to type conversion in Python (e.g., the `int()` function). Here's an example.

```
short int x, y=20;
long int z=3;

x=(short int)(y/z);
```

Note how you are directing the compiler to turn the division into a `short int`. Otherwise, the result is in fact a `long int` due to the promotion of y to the level of z. What's the value of x? Why it's 6 of course! Remember, the fractional part is meaningless, and thus lost, on integer divides.

Casting is also useful when using math functions. If you have to use `float`, you can cast them to/from `double` to make use of functions defined with `double`. For example, suppose a, b, and c are declared as `float` but you wish to use the `pow()` function to raise a to the b power. `pow()` is defined as taking two `double` arguments and returning a `double` answer.

```
c = (float)pow( (double)a, (double)b );
```

This is a very explicit example. Many times you can rely on a "silent cast" promotion to do your work for you as in the integer example above. Sometimes being explicit is a good practice just as a form of documentation.

4.4 Bitwise Operations

Sometimes you'd like to perform bitwise operations rather than ordinary math. For example, what if you want to logically AND two variables, bit by bit? Bitwise operations are very common when programming microcontrollers as a means of setting, clearing and testing specific bits in control registers (for example, setting a specific pin on a digital port to read mode instead of write mode). C has a series of bitwise operators. They are:

&	AND
|	OR
^	XOR
~	One's Complement
>>	Shift Right
<<	Shift Left

Figure 4.2, bitwise operators

Note the double use of & for "address of" and now AND. The unary operation is always "address of", and the binary operation is always AND, so a & b would **not** imply the address of b. If you wanted to AND x with y, shift the result 2 places to the left and assign the result to z, you'd use:

```
z = (x&y)<<2;
```

Let's look at a few examples. Suppose the variables X, Y and Z are unsigned chars. X and Y are set to 13 and 134, respectively. In hex, that's 0x0d and 0x86 for bit patterns of 00001101 and 10000110.

```
Z = X<<3;   // Z is 01101000 or 0x68
Z = X>>1;   // Z is 00000110 or 0x06
Z = ~X;     // Z is 11110010 or 0xf2
Z = X|Y;    // Z is 10001111 or 0x8f
Z = X&Y;    // Z is 00000100 or 0x04
Z = X^Y;    // Z is 10001011 or 0x8b
```

4.5 Setting, Clearing and Reading Register Bits

Bitwise operations may appear to be somewhat arcane to the uninitiated but are in fact commonly used. A prime use is in setting, clearing and testing specific bits in registers. One example involves configuring bidirectional ports for input or output mode via a *data direction register*, typically abbreviated DDR. Each bit of the DDR represents a specific output pin. A logic high might indicate output mode while a logic low would indicate input mode. Assuming DDR is an 8 bit register, if you wanted to set all bits except the 0th bit to input mode, you could write[5]:

```
DDR = 0x01; // set bit zero to output mode
```

---

[5] In C, bit position counting, like most sequences, starts from position 0 not position 1.

Embedded Controllers

If sometime later you wanted to also set the 1st and 2nd bits to output mode while keeping everything else intact, the easy way to do it is simply to OR the bits you want:

```
DDR = DDR | 0x06;
```

The prior operation may be performed using the more common shorthand:

```
DDR |= 0x06;
```

Note that the preceding code does not affect any of the other bits so they stay in whatever mode they were originally. By the way, a set of specific bits (such as the 0x06 above) is often referred to as a *bit pattern* or *bitmask*.

To see if a specific bit is set, simply AND instead of OR. So, to see if the 1st bit of DDR is set for output mode, you could use something like:

```
if ( DDR & 0x02 )        // true if set
```

Clearing bits requires ANDing with a bitmask that has been complemented. In other words, all 1s and 0s have been reversed in the bit pattern. If, for example, we want to clear the 0th and 4th bits, we'd first complement the bit pattern 0x11 yielding 0xee. Then we AND:

```
DDR &= 0xee;
```

Often, it's easier to just use the logical complement operator on the original bit pattern and then AND it:

```
DDR &= (~0x11);
```

If you're dealing with a single bit, you can use the left shift operator so you don't even have to bother figuring out the bit pattern in hex. To set the 3rd bit and then clear the 4th bit of DDR, you could use the following:

```
DDR |=  (0x01<<3);
DDR &= ~(0x01<<4);
```

These operations are so common that they are often invoked using an in-line expansion via a `#define`.

4.6 #define

Very often it is desirable to use symbolic constants in place of actual values. For example, you'd probably prefer to use a symbol such as PI instead of the number 3.14159. You can do this with the `#define` preprocessor directive. These are normally found in header files (such as stdio.h or math.h) or at the top of a module of C source code. You might see something like:

```
#define PI 3.14159
```

Once the compiler sees this, every time it comes across the token `PI` it will replace it with the value 3.14159. This directive uses a simple substitution but you can do many more complicated things than this. For example, you can also create something that looks like a function:

```
#define parallel((x),(y))    ((x)*(y))/((x)+(y))
```

The `x` and `y` serve as placeholders. Thus, the line

```
a = parallel( b, c );
```

gets expanded to:

```
a = (a*b)/(a+b);
```

Why do this? Because it's an *in-line expansion* or *macro*. That means that there's no function call overhead and the operation runs faster. At the same time, it reads like a function, so it's easier for a programmer to follow. OK, but why all the extra parentheses? The reason is because x and y are placeholders, and those items might be expressions, not simple variables. If you did it this way you might get in trouble:

```
#define parallel(x,y)   x*y/(x+y)
```

What if x is an expression, as in the following example?

```
a = parallel(2+b,c);
```

This would expand to:

```
a = 2+b*c/(2+b+c);
```

As multiplication is executed before addition, you wind up with 2 being added to the product of b times c *after* the division, which is not the same as the sum of 2 and b being multiplied by c, and that quantity then being divided. By using the extra parentheses, the order of execution is maintained.

Referring back to the bit field operations, here are some useful definitions for what appear to be functions but which are, in fact, bitwise operations expanded in-line:

```
#define bitRead(value, bit)   (((value) >> (bit)) & 0x01)
#define bitSet(value, bit)    ((value) |= (1UL << (bit)))
#define bitClear(value, bit)  ((value) &= ~(1UL << (bit)))
```

The `1UL` simply means 1 expressed as an unsigned long. Finally, `bit` could also be defined as a symbol which leads to some nice looking self-documenting code:

```
#define LEDBIT 7

// more code here...

bitSet( DDR, LEDBIT );
```

`#define` expansions can get quite tricky because they can have nested references. This means that one `#define` may contain within it a symbol which is itself a `#define`. Following these can be a little tedious at times but ultimately are worth the effort. We shall look at a few down the road. Remember, these are done to make day-to-day programming easier, not to obfuscate the code. For now, start with simple math constant substitutions. They are extremely useful and easy to use. Just keep in the back of your mind that, with microcontrollers, specific registers and ports are often given symbolic names such as

PORTB so that you don't have to remember the precise numeric addresses of them. The norm is to place these symbolic constants in ALL CAPS.

4.7 Keywords

Here is a list of keywords in the C language:

```
auto        break       case        char        const
continue    do          default     double      else
entry       extern      float       for         goto
if          int         long        register    return
sizeof      short       static      struct      switch
typedef     union       unsigned    volatile    while
```

Figure 4.3, C language keywords

We've looked at quite a few of these already. Some that we haven't you can probably guess the use of. As stated previously, C is a "skinny" language!

4.8 Exercises

1. Write a line of code that will print the statement "The result is x volts" where x is the value given by the floating point variable `output_voltage`.

2. Write a line of code to define a constant called `RECIP2PI` that is equal to $1/(2\pi)$.

3. Write the code to determine the number of bytes required for a variable called `POWER_SUPPLY`.

4. Assume the 8 bit variable `X` exists. Write the code to set the MSB (most significant bit), leaving all other bits unchanged.

5. Assume the 8 bit variable `Y` exists. Write the code to set the LSB (least significant bit), leaving all other bits unchanged.

6. Assume the 8 bit variable `Z` exists. Write the code to clear the MSB and LSB, leaving all other bits unchanged.

7. Assume the 8 bit variable `W` exists. Write the code to complement each bit (flip 0 to 1 and 1 to 0).

8. If `X` is 0x04 and `Y` is 0x09, what are a) `X|Y`, b) `X&Y`, c) `~X`, d) `0xf1&Y`?

9. If `X` is 0xf0 and `Y` is 0x11, what are a) `X|Y`, b) `X&Y`, c) `~X`, d) `0xf1&Y`?

5. C Storage Types and Scope

5.1 Types

C has several ways of storing or referencing variables. These affect the way variables behave. Some of the more common ones are: auto, register, and static.

Auto variables are variables declared within functions that are not static or register types. That is, the `auto` keyword is the default. Normally, auto variables are created on the application's stack, although C doesn't require this. The stack is basically a chunk of memory that is allocated for the application's use when it is first run. It is a place for temporary storage, with values popped onto and pulled off of the stack in first-in, last-out order (like a stack of plates). Unless you initialize an auto variable, you have no idea what its value is when you first use it. Its value happens to be whatever was in that memory location the previous time it was used. It is important to understand that this includes subsequent calls to a function (i.e., its prior value is not "remembered" the next time you call the function). This is because any subsequent call to a function does not have to produce the same the memory locations for these variables, anymore than you always wind up with the same plate every time you go to the cafeteria.

Register variables are similar to auto types in behavior, but instead of using the usual stack method, a CPU register is used (if available). The exact implementation is CPU and compiler specific. In some case the `register` keyword is ignored and a simple auto type is used. CPU registers offer faster access than normal memory so register variables are used to create faster execution of critical code. Typically this includes counters or pointers that are incremented inside of loops. A declaration would like something like this:

```
register int x;
```

Static variables are used when you need a variable that maintains its value between function calls. So, if we need a variable that will "appear the way we left it" from the last call, we might use something like this:

```
static char y;
```

There is one important difference between auto and static types concerning initialization. If an auto variable is initialized in a function as so:

```
char a=1;
```

Then `a` is set to 1 each time the function is entered. If you do the same initialization with a static, as in:

```
static char b=1;
```

Then `b` is set to 1 **only** on the first call. Subsequent entries into the function would not incur the initialization. If it did reinitialize, what would be the sense of having a static type? This is explained by the fact that a static does not usually use the stack method of storage, but rather is placed at a fixed memory location. Again, C does not *require* the use of a stack, rather, it is a typical implementation.

Two useful but not very common modifiers are `volatile` and `const`. A `volatile` variable is one that can be accessed or modified by another process or task. This has some very special uses (typically, to prevent an optimizing compiler from being too aggressive with optimizations-more on this later). The `const` modifier is used for declaring constants, that is, variables that should not change value. In some instances this is preferred over using `#define` as type checking is now available (but you can't use the two interchangeably).

5.2 Scope

Scope has to do with where variables are "seen". We have already mentioned the idea of global and local in previous work but it is time to delve a little deeper. Generally, variables only exist within the block they are declared. While it is legal to declare variables inside of a conditional or loop block, we normally declare variables at the very beginning of a function. Consequently, these variables are known within the function. That is, their scope of reference is within the function. Nothing outside of the function knows anything about them. Thus, we say that they are local, or perhaps localized, to the function. For example, consider the two function fragments below:

```
void func1( void )
{
    int x;
    int y;
    //...some code here...
}

void func2( void )
{
    int y;
    int z;
    //...some other code here...
}
```

There is no direct way to access the `z` variable of `func2()` from `func1()`. Likewise, there is no direct way to access the `x` variable of `func1()` from `func2()`. More interestingly, the `y` variables of `func1()` and `func2()` are entirely different! They do **not** refer to the same variable. This sometimes can be confusing for new programmers but it is essential for large programs. Imagine that you were working with a team of people on a very large program, perhaps tens of thousands of lines long. If the idea of local scope did not exist, you'd have to make sure that every single variable in the program had a unique name! This would create a nightmare of confusion. By using local scope, you're saying: "I only need this variable for a job within this function. As it only needs to exist within this function, its name is only meaningful within this function."

If some form of "universally known" data item is needed, we can resort to the *global*. Globals act pretty much like statics and are usually stored the same way. If you have a program that consists of a single file, you can declare your globals by listing them at the beginning of the program before (and outside of) any functions. In this way they will be read by the compiler first and will therefore be "known" to all functions that follow. Do not get in the habit of declaring all variables as global. This is considered a bad and inefficient coding method. Get into the habit of using locals as the norm and resort to globals only when called for.

If you have a multiple file project, how do you get the functions in the second file to recognize the globals declared in the first file? In this case, you'll create a header file and use the `#include` directive. For example, suppose your project consists of two C source files named foo.c and bar.c.

In foo.c you declare the following global:

```
int m;
```

In order for the functions in bar.c to "see" m, you'll create a header file, perhaps called foo.h. foo.h will contain the following:

```
extern int m;
```

Meaning that an integer named m has been declared externally (i.e., in another file). At the top of bar.c you'll add the line:

```
#include <foo.h>
```

So, when bar.c is compiled, the compiler will first open up foo.h. It will see that the variable m has been declared elsewhere and puts it in a "known variables list". It then continues to compile the remainder of you code. When it comes across m in some function, the compiler "understands" that this is a variable that was declared in another file. No problem!

So, you can now see that header files are largely composed of definitions and declarations from other places, namely external data and function prototypes.

5.4 Exercises

1. Assume a function declares a variable like so: `static int x=0;` The function increments the variable and then prints its value. What does the function print out on the tenth call to the function? How would this change if the `static` keyword was not used?

2. Consider the following snippet of code:

```
void doug( void )
{
    int x=0;

    x=x+1;
    printf( "%d\n", x );
}
void dinsdale( void )
{
    int x=20;

    x=x+1;
    printf( "%d\n", x );
}
```

Suppose you call `doug()` five times in a row and then call `dinsdale()` five times in a row. What would the resulting output look like?

6. C Arrays and Strings

6.1 Introduction

Up to now we haven't talked much about character strings, that is, variables that contain non-numeric data such as a person's name or address. There is no string variable type in C (unlike Python). In C, strings are nothing more than arrays of characters. Arrays are a simple grouping of like variables in a sequence, each with the same name and accessed via an index number. They behave similarly to arrays in most other languages (or lists in Python). C arrays may have one, two, or more dimensions. Here are a few example declarations:

```
float results[10];       An array of 10 floats
long int x[20];          An array of 20 longs, or 80 bytes
char y[10][15];          A two-dimension array, 10 by 15 chars each, 150 bytes total
```

Note the use of square brackets and the use of multiple sets of square brackets for higher dimension arrays. Also, C arrays are counted from index 0 rather than 1.[6] For example, the first item of `results[]` is `results[0]`. The last item is `results[9]`. There is no such item here as `results[10]`. That would constitute an illegal access. You can pre-initialize arrays by listing values within braces, each separated by a comma:

```
double a[5] = {1.0, 2.0, 4.7, -177.0, 6.3e4};
```

If you leave the index out, you get as many elements as you initialize:

```
short int b[] = {1, 5, 6, 7}; /* four elements */
```

If you declare more than you initialize, the remainder are set to zero if the array is global or static (but not if auto).

```
short int c[10] = {1, 3, 20}; /* remaining 7 are set to 0 */
```

If you are dealing with character strings you could enter the ASCII codes for the characters, but this would be tedious in most cases. C let's you specify the character in single quotes and it will do the translation:

```
char m[20] = {'m', 'y', ' ', 'd', 'o', 'g', 0};
```

(The reason for the trailing 0 will be evident in a moment.) Even easier is to specify the string within double quotes:

```
char n[20]={"Bill the cat"};
```

Consider the string `n[]` above. It contains 12 characters but was declared to hold 20. Why do this? Well, you may need to copy some other string into this variable at a future time. By declaring a larger value, the variable can hold a larger string later. At this point you might be wondering how the C library functions "know" to use just a portion of the allocated space at any given time (in this case, just the first 12

---

[6] The reason for this will be apparent when we cover addresses and pointers.

characters). This is possible through a simple rule: **All strings must be null terminated.** That is, the character after the final character in use must be null, numerically 0. In the case of the direct string initialization of `n[]`, the null is automatically added after the final character, *t*. In the case of the character-by-character initialization of `m[]`, we had to do it manually. The null is extremely important. Functions that manipulate or print strings look for the trailing null in order to determine when their work is done. Without a null termination, the functions will just churn through memory until they eventually hit a null, which may cause system violations and even application or operating system crashes. Note that

```
char my_pet[] = {"fido"};
```

actually declares five characters, not four (four letters plus the terminating null). As C counts from index 0, this declaration is equivalent to:

```
my_pet[0]= 'f';
my_pet[1]= 'i';
my_pet[2]= 'd';
my_pet[3]= 'o';
my_pet[4]=  0;
```

The trailing null may also be written as '\0'. It is important to note that without the backslash, this has an entirely different meaning! '\0' means null, but '0' means the numeral 0.

6.2 String Manipulation

A confusing aspect of C strings for beginners (especially those coming from BASIC or even Python) is how to manipulate them. That is, how do you copy one string to another, compare strings, extract a substring, and so forth? As strings are really arrays, you can't assign one to the other as in `a[] = b[];` Instead, we rely on a series of string functions found in the string library. To use these functions, you need to link your code with the string library and use `#include <string.h>` at the start of your code. To copy one string to another, use `strcpy()`. The template is:

```
strcpy( destination, source );
```

So, if you wanted to copy the contents of `my_pet[]` into `n[]`, you could write:

```
strcpy( &n[0], &my_pet[0] );
```

If you're awake at this point, you might ask "What's with the ampersand?" Good question! What the string copy function needs are the starting addresses of the two arrays. In essence, all it does is copy a character at a time from the source to the destination. When it hits the trailing null it's done. We've already seen the "address of" (`&`) operator earlier when we looked at `scanf()`. So, all we're saying here is "For the source, start at the address of the first character of `my_pet[]`, and for the destination, start at the first character of `n[]`." This can be a little cumbersome, so C offers a shortcut. You can think of `&` and `[]` as sort of canceling each other out. We'd normally write:

```
strcpy( n, my_pet );
```

Note that it is perfectly acceptable to use an index other than zero if you need to copy over just a chunk of the string. You could start copying from index 2 if you'd like, and just get "do" instead of "fido":

```
        strcpy( n, &my_pet[2] );
```

This can also be shortcut by using:

```
        strcpy( n, my_pet+2 );
```

that is, don't start at the address of the first element of `my_pet[]`, start 2 characters later. We'll look at this sort of manipulation much closer when we examine addresses and pointers.

What happens if the source string has more characters than the destination string was allocated to? For example, what if you did this?

```
        strcpy( my_pet, n );
```

This results in a memory overwrite that can accidentally destroy other variables or functions. Very bad! Your program may crash, and in some cases, your operating system my crash. To protect against this, you can use `strncpy()`. This places a limit on the number of characters copied by adding a third argument. As the destination only has space for 5 characters, you'd use:

```
        strncpy( my_pet, n, 5 );
```

This function will stop at 5 characters. Unfortunately, it won't automatically null terminate the string if the limit is reached. To be safe, you'd need to add the following line:

```
        my_pet[4] = 0; /* force null termination */
```

Remember, as C counts from 0, index 4 is the fifth (and final) element. There are many functions available to manipulate strings as well as individual characters. Here is a short list:

`strcmp()`	Compares two strings (alphabetically)
`strcmpi()`	As above, but case insensitive
`strncmp()`	Compares two strings with max length
`strncat()`	Concatenate two strings with max length
`strlen()`	Find length of string (count of chars before null)

Figure 6.1, string functions

The following work on single characters. Again this is just a sampling to give you an idea of what's out there. Use `#include <ctype.h>`

`isupper()`	Determines if character is upper case
`isalpha()`	Determines if character is alphabetic (not numeral, punctuation, etc.)
`tolower()`	Turns character into lower case version

Figure 6.2, character functions

If you don't have library documentation, it can be very instructive to simply open various header files and look at the function prototypes to see what's available. Whatever you do though, **don't edit these files!**

Finally, if you need to convert numeric strings into integer or floating point values, use the functions `atoi()`, `atol()` and `atof()`. (ASCII to int or long int in stdlib.h, ASCII to float in math.h).

6.3 Exercises

1. Write the code to declare an array of 12 single precision real numbers.

2. Write the code to declare an array of 15 eight bit signed integers.

3. Assume that an array of 100 double precision real numbers has been declared and is named `points`. Write the code to print out the first item of `points`. Also, write the code to set the last item of `points` to 0.0.

4. Declare a string called `mammal` and initialize it to the word *woodchuck*.

5. Do you see any potential problems with this snippet of initialization code? If so, explain the issues and how they might be corrected.

```
char bird;

bird[0]='s'
bird[1]='w'
bird[2]='a'
bird[3]='l'
bird[4]='l'
bird[5]='o'
bird[6]='w'
```

7. C Conditionals and Looping

7.1 Conditionals

C uses a fairly standard if/else construct for basic conditionals. They may be nested and each portion may consist of several statements. The condition itself may have multiple elements and be formed in either positive or negative logic. The basic construct is:

```
if( test condition(s)... )
{
        //...do stuff...
}
```

The else portion is optional and looks like:

```
if( test condition(s).. )
{
        //...do stuff...
}
else
{
        //...do other stuff...
}
```

If there is only a single statement in the block (i.e., between the braces), the braces may be removed if desired:

```
if( test condition(s).. )
        //...single statement...
else
        //...do other statement...
```

The test condition may check for numerous possibilities. The operators are:

==	equality
!=	inequality
>	greater than
<	less than
>=	greater than or equal to
<=	less than or equal to

Figure 7.1, relational operators

It is very important to note that equality uses a double equal sign. A single equal sign is an assignment operation. Don't think "equals", think "same as", with one symbol for each word. You may also use Boolean (logic) operators, as shown in Figure 7.2.

||	OR
&&	AND
!	NOT

Figure 7.2, logical operators

Note that the logical operators do **not** behave the same as the similarly named bitwise operators. For example, a logical AND returns TRUE if its two arguments are non-zero, not necessarily the same bits. That is 1 & 2 yields 0, but 1 && 2 yields TRUE. **TRUE is taken to be any non-zero value.** Any variable or expression that evaluates to a value other than zero is logically TRUE. If the result is zero, then it is logically FALSE. Time for some examples. The conditional is written as a fragment with an explanation following:

```
if( a==6 )
        /* taken only if the variable a is a 6 */

if( b!=7 )
        /* taken as long as the variable b isn't 7 */

if( (a==6) && (b!=7) )
        /* taken as long as a is 6 and b is something other than 7 */

if( (a==6) || (b!=7) )
        /* taken as long as a is 6 or b is something other than 7 */

if( a==0 )
        /* taken if a is zero */

if( !a )
        /* another way of saying taken if a is zero */

if( a!=0 )
        /* taken if a is not zero */

if( a )
        /* another way of saying taken if a is not zero */
```

How you word something is up to you. The following two code fragments are equivalent:

```
if( a==b )
        do_x();
else
        do_y();

if( a!=b )
        do_y();
else
        do_x();
```

It is very common for new programmers to use = when they want ==. This can have disastrous results. Consider the following code fragment:

Embedded Controllers

```
if( a=b )
```

What does this do? At first glance, you might think it tests to see if `a` and `b` are the same. It does nothing of the kind! Instead, it assigns the value of `b` to `a` and then checks to see if that value is non-zero. In other words, it does this:

```
a=b;
if( a )
```

A trick to help you with this, at least with constants, is to reverse the normal order. Instead of writing `if( a==6 )`, use `if( 6==a )`. This way, if you accidentally use a single equal sign, the compiler will cough up a syntax error.

7.2 Nesting

If a multiple condition won't cut it, you can nest if/else tests. Nesting conditionals is easy:

```
if( test condition(s).. )
{
    if( other tests.. )
    {
    }
    else
    {
    }
}
else
{
    if( still other tests.. )
    {
    }
    else
    {
    }
}
```

You can go many levels deep if you desire. Note that C, unlike Python, doesn't *require* the indenting shown, but it is expected formatting. For selection of a single value out of a list, you can use the switch/case construct. The template looks like:

```
switch( test_variable )
{
    case value_1:
        //...do stuff...
        break;
    case value_2:
        //...do other stuff...
        break;
    default:
        //...do stuff for a value not in the list...
        break;
}
```

The `default` section is optional. Also, it does not have to be the final item in the list. If a `break` is left out, the code will simply fall through to the next case, otherwise code execution jumps to the closing brace. Also, cases can be stacked together. The action statements for each case may include any legal statements including assignments, function calls, `if/else`, other `switch/case`, and so on. Note that you cannot check for ranges, nor can the cases be expressions. The cases must be discrete values. The following example shows all of these. The action statements are replaced with simple comments.

```
switch( x )
{
    case 1:
        /* This code performed only if x is 1, then jump to closing
           brace */
        break;

    case 2:
        /* This code performed only if x is 2, then jump to closing
           brace */
        break;

    case 3:
        /* This code performed only if x is 3, but continue to next
           case (no break statement) */
    case 4:
    case 5:
        /* This code performed only if x is 3, 4, or 5,  */
        break;

    default:
        /* this code performed only if x is not any of 1,2,3,4, or
             5, then jump to closing brace (redundant here) */
        break;
}
```

Sometimes it is very handy to replace the numeric constants with `#define` values. For example, you might be choosing from a menu of different circuits. You would create some `#define` values for each at the start of the file (or in a header file) as so:

```
#define VOLTAGE_DIVIDER      1
#define EMITTER_FEEDBACK     2
#define COLLECTOR_FEEDBACK   3
/* etc... */
```

You would then write a much more legible switch/case like so:

```
switch( bias_choice )
{
    case VOLTAGE_DIVIDER:
        /* do volt div stuff */
        break;

    case EMITTER_FEEDBACK:
        /* do emit fdbk stuff */
        break;
    /* and so on... */
}
```

7.3 Looping

There are three looping constructs in C. They are `while()`, `do-while()`, and `for()`. `do-while()` is really just a `while()` with the loop continuation test at the end instead of the beginning. Therefore, you always get at least one iteration. The continuation test follows the same rules as the `if()` construct. Here are the `while()` and `do-while()` templates:

```
while( test condition(s)... )
{
      //...statements to iterate...
}

do {
      //..statements to iterate...
} while( test condition(s)... )
```

Here are some examples:

```
while( a<10 )
{
    /* Perhaps a is incremented in here.
       If a starts off at 10 or more, this loop never executes */
}

do {
    /* Perhaps a is incremented in here.
       If a starts off at 10 or more, this loop executes once */
} while( a<10 )

while( a<10 && b )
{
    /* This loop continues until a is 10 or more, or b is zero.
       Either condition will halt the loop. Variable a must be
       less than 10 and b must be non-zero for the loop to
       continue */
}
```

Usually, loops use some form of counter. The obvious way to implement a counter is with a statement like:

```
a=a+1;      /* add one to the current value of a */
```

C has increment and decrement operators, ++ and --, so you can say things like:

```
a++;    /* add one to the current value of a */
a--;    /* subtract one from the current value of a */
```

C also has a shortcut mode for most operations. Here are two examples:

```
a+=1; /* equivalent to a=a+1; or a++; */
a*=2; /* equivalent to a=a*2; */
```

You will see all three forms of increment in example and production code, although the increment and decrement operators are generally preferred.

The `for()` construct is generally preferred over the `while()` if a specific number of iterations are known. The template is:

```
for( initialization(s); termination test(s); increment(s) )
{
        ..statements to iterate..
}
```

Here is an example using the variable a as a counter that starts at 0 and proceeds to 9 by adding one each time. The loop iterates 10 times.

```
for( a=0; a<10; a++ )
{
        /* stuff to do ten times */
}
```

The following example is similar, but adds 2 at each loop, thus iterating 5 times.

```
for( a=0; a<10; a+=2 )
{
        /* stuff to do five times */
}
```

The next example uses multiples. Note the use of commas.

```
for( a=0, b=1; a<10; a++, b*=3 )
{
        /* stuff to do ten times */
}
```

In this case two variables are initialized. Also, at each loop completion, a is incremented by 1 and b is multiplied by 3. Note that b is not used in the termination section, although it could be.

If the iterated block within the braces consists of only a single statement, the braces may be left out (just like in the `if/else` construct). Loops may be nested and contain any legal C statements including assignments, conditionals, function calls and the like. They may also be terminated early through the use of the break statement. As in the `switch/case` construct, the `break` command redirects program flow to the closing brace. Here is an example:

```
for( a=0, b=2; a<7; a++ )
{
      while( b<a*10 )
            b*=2;

      if( b > 50 )
            break;
}
```

Embedded Controllers

Note that the `if()` is not part of the `while()`. This is visually reinforced by the use of indents and spacing, but that's not what makes it so. The code would behave the same even if it was entered like so:

```
for( a=0, b=2; a<7; a++ ){ while( b<a*10 ) b*=2; if( b>50 ) break;}
```

Obviously, the former style is much easier to read than the later. It is **strongly** recommended that you follow the first style when you write code.

OK, what does the code fragment do? First, it sets `a` to 0 and `b` to 2. Then, the `while()` checks to see if `b` is less than 10 times `a`. 2 is not less than 0, so the `while()` doesn't iterate. Next, the `if()` checks to see if `b` is more than 50. It's not, so the `break` isn't executed. That concludes the first iteration. For the second iteration, `a` is incremented to 1 and checked to see if it's still less than 7. It is, so the loop continues and enters the `while()`. `b` is smaller than 10 times `a` (2<10), so `b` is doubled to 4. This is still smaller so it's doubled again to 4, and again to 8. Finally, it is doubled to 16. It is now larger than 10 times `a` so the `while()` loop exits. The `if()` isn't true as 16 is not larger than 50 so the `break` isn't taken. We wind up finishing iteration two by incrementing `a` to 2. The `while()` loop starts because `b` (16) is less than 10 times `a` (now 20). The loop will only execute once, leaving `b` at 32. This is still less than 50, so the `break` is ignored. The `for()` closes by incrementing `a` to 3. On the next iteration both the `while()` and `if()` are ignored as `b` is less than 10 times `a` as well less than 50. All that happens as that `a` is incremented to 4. Now that `a` is 4, the `while()` starts again (32<40). `b` is doubled to 64. That's greater than 10 times `a`, so the `while()` exits. `b` is now greater than 50 so the `if()` is taken. This results in executing the `break` statement that directs program flow to the closing brace of the `for()` loop. Execution picks up at the line following the closing brace and we are all done with the `for()` loop (no, `a` never gets to 7). This example is admittedly a little tricky to follow and not necessarily the best coding practice, but it does illustrate how the various parts operate.

7.4 While or For?

So, which do you use, a `while()` or a `for()`? You can make simple loops with either of them but `for()` loops are handy in that the initialization, termination, and increment are all in one spot. With `while()` loops, you only specify the termination, so you must remember to write the variable initializations before the loop as well as the increments within the loop. If you forget either of these your loop will behave erratically. It may fail to terminate altogether, resulting in an infinite loop, as shown below.

```
a=0;

while( a<10 )
{
        printf("hello\n");
}
```

This code fragment doesn't print the word *hello* ten times, it prints *hello* forever (or better to say until you forcibly terminate the program)! Although `a` was initialized and tested, it was never incremented. You need an `a++;` (or similar) within that loop.

7.5 Exercises

1. Write the code to examine the value of the variable X. If it's less than zero, the message *negative value* should be printed.

2. Write the code to examine the value of the variable X. If it's equal to zero, the message *zero value* should be printed.

3. Write the code to compare the values of the variables X and Y. The greater value should be printed.

4. Write the code to examine the values of the variables X and Y. If both X and Y are greater than zero, increment X by one.

5. Write the code necessary to print the message *Error!* six times but without using six sequential `printf()` calls.

6. Write the code required to control a loop so that it continues so long as the variable K is less than 50.

7. Write the code needed to cycle the variable R from 100 to 200 in steps of 5 (i.e., 100, 105, 110, etc.).

8. Explain the practical difference between a `while` loop and a `do-while` loop.

8. C Pointers and Addresses

8.1 Introduction

As you may recall from earlier course work, every byte of memory in a computer system is identified by a unique address. C works directly with addresses and this is one reason why it can be used to create efficient and powerful code. You can obtain the address of virtually any variable or data item using the "address of" operator, &. One exception to this is the `register` class variable. This is because CPU's registers don't have an address like normal memory. Also, as functions are just memory locations filled with microprocessor/microcontroller op-codes, C also makes it possible to obtain the starting address of functions.

8.2 Using Addresses and Pointers

If we declare a variable as so:

```
char a;
```

then referencing `a` will get us the value stored in `a`, as in the code `b=a;`. Using the *address of* operator, as in `&a`, will obtain the memory location of `a`, not `a`'s value or contents. This is the sort of thing we used with `scanf()` and `strcpy()`. It is possible to declare variables that are designed to hold these addresses. They are called *pointers*. To declare a pointer, you preface the variable with an asterisk like so:

```
char *pc;
```

The variable `pc` is not a `char`, it is a pointer to a `char`. That is, its contents are the address of a `char` variable. The content of *any* pointer is an address. This is a very important point. Consider the following code fragments based on the declarations above:

```
pc = a;     /* unhappy */
pc = &a;    /* just fine */
```

The first line makes no sense as we are trying to assign apples to oranges, so to speak. The second line makes perfect sense as both `pc` and `&a` are the same sort of thing, namely the address of a variable that holds a `char`. What if we want pointers to other kinds of things? No problem, just follow the examples below:

```
float *pf;          /* pointer to a float */
long int *pl;       /* pointer to a long int */
double *pd, *p2;    /* two pointers to doubles */
short int *ps, i;   /* ps is a pointer to a short int */
                    /* i is just a short int */
```

As mentioned, all pointers contain addresses. Therefore, **no matter what the pointer points to, all pointers are the same size (same number of bytes)**. In most modern systems, pointers are either 32 bits (4 bytes) or 64 bits (8 bytes) although some small controllers use 16 bit addressing. When in doubt, you can check your code with `sizeof()`. If all pointers are the same size, then why do we declare different types of pointers? There are two reasons. First, this helps with type checking. Functions that take pointers as arguments or that return pointers will be using certain forms of data. You wouldn't want to accidentally send off a pointer to a `float` when the function expects the address of a `short int` for example. Second, by specifying the type of thing the pointer points to, we can rely on the compiler to generate proper *pointer math* (more on this in a moment).

8.3 Pointer Dereferencing

Suppose you have the following code fragment:

```
char *pc, c, b;

c = 1;
pc = &c;
```

We have declared two variables, a `char` and a pointer to a `char`. We then set the contents of the `char` to 1, and set the contents of the pointer to the address of the `char`. We don't really need to know what this address is, but for the sake of argument, let's say that c is located at memory address 2000 while pc is located at memory address 3000. If we were to search the computer's memory, at address 2000 we would find the number 1. At address 3000, we would find the number 2000, that is, the address of the `char` variable. In a typical system, this value could span 32 bits or 4 bytes. In other words, the memory used by pc is addresses 3000, 3001, 3002, and 3003. Conversely, in a 16 bit system, pc would only span 3000 and 3001 (half as many bytes, but far fewer possible addresses).

As the contents of (i.e., value of) pc tell us where a `char` resides, we can get to that location, and thus the value of the `char` variable c. To do this, we *dereference* the pointer with an asterisk. We could say:

```
b = *pc;
```

Read this as "b gets the value at the address given by pc". That is, pc doesn't give us the value, rather, it tells us where to go to get the value. It's as if you went to your professor's office and asked for your grade, and instead he hands you a piece of paper that reads "I will e-mail it to you". The paper doesn't indicate your grade, but it shows you where to find it. This might sound unduly complicated at first but it turns out to have myriad uses. By the way, in this example the value of b will be 1 because pc points to c, which was assigned the value 1 at the start. That is, b gets the value at the address pc points to, which is simply c.

8.4 Pointer Math

One of the really neat things about pointers is pointer math. Returning to our example of pc at address 3000, if you increment pc, as in pc++; you'll get 3001. No surprise, right? If, on the other hand, you had a pointer to a `double`, pd, at address 3000 and you incremented it, you wouldn't wind up with 3001. In fact, you'd wind up with 3008. Why? This comes down to how large the thing is that we're pointing at. `doubles` are 8 bytes each. If you had a bunch of them, as in an array, incrementing the pointer would get you the next item in the array. This is extremely useful. Note that adding and subtracting to/from pointers makes perfect sense, but multiplying, dividing, and higher manipulations generally make no sense and are to be avoided.

8.5 Pointers and Arrays

We very often use pointers with arrays. One example is the use of strings. We noted this in earlier work. Recall that the "address of" and array index "cancel each other" so that the following are equivalent:

```
&somestring[0]     somestring
```

Let's look at an example of how you might use pointers instead of normal array indexing. We shall write our own version of `strcpy()` to copy one string to another. The function takes two arguments, the address of a source string and the address of a destination string. We will copy over a character at a time until we come to the null termination. First, the normal array index way:

```
void strcpy1( char dest[], char source[] )
{
    int i=0;                        /* index variable, init to first char */

    while( source[i] != 0 )         /* if it's not null...*/
    {
        dest[i] = source[i];        /* copy the char */
        i++;                        /* increment index */
    }
    dest[i] = 0;                    /* null terminate */
}
```

Looks pretty straightforward, right? There are some minor improvements you can make such as changing the loop to `while( source[i] )`, but that's not a big deal. Now in contrast, let's write the same thing using pointers.

```
void strcpy2( char *dest, char *source )
{
    while( *dest++ = *source++ );
}
```

That's it. Here's how it works. `dest` and `source` are the starting addresses of the strings. If you say:

```
*dest = *source;
```

then what happens is that the value that `source` points to gets copied to the address referred to by `dest`. That copies one character. Now, to this we add the post increment operator ++:

```
*dest++ = *source++;
```

This line copies the first character as above and then increments each pointer. Thus, each pointer contains the address of the next character in the array (you've got to love that pointer math, this will work with any sized datum). By placing this code within the `while()` loop, if the content (i.e., the character copied) is non-zero, the loop will continue. The loop won't stop until the terminating null has been copied. As you can imagine, the underlying machine code for `strcpy2()` will be much simpler, more compact, and faster to execute than that of `strcpy1()`. As was said at the outset of the course, you can do a lot in C with just a little code!

8.6 Exercises

1. Declare a pointer to a floating point variable, naming it `fptr`.

2. Declare a pointer to a signed character variable, naming it `cptr`.

3. Consider the following snippet of code:

    ```
    unsigned char c, *p;
    ```

    Explain the difference between c and p.

4. Consider the following snippet of code:

    ```
    unsigned char *p;
    double *p2;
    ```

    Assume that the value of p is currently 1000 and the value of p2 is 2000. What are their values after the following piece of code is executed?

    ```
    p++;
    p2++;
    ```

5. Explain the difference between the * and & operators in relation to pointers.

6. Consider the line of code below.

    ```
    a = b*c;
    ```

    Is the * operator a pointer dereference or a multiply? How do we know?

7. Consider the line of code below.

    ```
    a = b**c;
    ```

    What do you think this line does? How might you alter this line to mark the intent more clearly and less prone to error or misinterpretation?

8. Explain the difference between the two lines of code below.

    ```
    a*=b;
    a=*b;
    ```

9. C Look-up Tables

9.1 Introduction

Sometimes we use tools to make things without thinking about how the tools themselves are made. In the world of software, sometimes *how* things are done (the implementation) can have a huge impact on performance. It turns out that sometimes we can trade performance in one area for another. For example, a certain technique might be very memory efficient but rather slow to execute, or vice versa. We're going to take a look at a common programming technique that is very fast (i.e., it's "computationally efficient"). Sometimes it can require a lot of memory, sometimes not. It's called a look-up table.

9.2 "Yes, I'd Like a Table for 360, Please"

Consider the common C trig function, `sin()`. Not much to it, really. You pass it an argument and you get back the sine of the argument. But how is it implemented? It could be implemented as a Taylor Series expansion that requires several multiplies and adds. A single sine computation won't take long but what if you need to do millions of them? All of those multiplies and adds add up, so to speak. Consider the following problem: You need to get the sine of an angle specified to the nearest degree, and *fast*. Basically, you have 360 possible answers (0 degrees through 359 degrees)[7]. Now suppose you create an array of 360 values which consists of the sine of each angle in one degree increments, starting at 0 degrees and working up to 359 degrees. It might look something like this:

```
double sine_table[] = { 0.0, 0.01745, 0.034899,  0.05234,
/* and so on to the last entry */ -0.01745 };
```

You can now "compute" the sine like so, given the argument `angle`:

```
answer = sine_table[ angle ];
```

Because of the duality of arrays and pointers, you can also write this as:

```
answer = *(sine_table + angle);
```

Without an optimizing compiler, the second form will probably generate more efficient machine code. In either case, this is very fast because it's nothing more than reading from a memory location with an offset. The result is just one add plus the access instead of a dozen multiply/adds. It does come at the cost of 360 double floats, which, at eight bytes each, is nearly 3k of memory. By recognizing that the sine function has quarter wave symmetry, you can add a little code to check for the quadrant and reduce the table to just 90 entries. Also, `floats` might have sufficient precision for the application which will cut the memory requirements in half again when compared to `doubles`.

---

[7] Outside those bounds you can always perform some minor integer math to get within the bounds (e.g., if the angle is 370, just mod by 360 to get the remainder of 10 degrees, effectively the "wrap around").

To make the above just a little spiffier, you can always make it look like a function via a `#define` as follows:

```
#define fast_sin(a)    (*(sine_table+(a)))
```

Of course, a down side to this operation is that it only deals with an integer argument and is only accurate to a single degree. You can alter the definition to allow a floating point argument and round it to the nearest whole degree as follows:

```
#define fast_sin(a)    (*(sine_table+(int)((a)+0.5)))
```

You could also turn this into a true function and add code to interpolate between adjacent whole degree entries for a more accurate result. At some point the extra refinements will slow the function to the point where a more direct computation becomes competitive.

9.3 Waving Quickly

So what's all this business about needing to do this sort of thing very fast? One application might be the direct digital synthesis of arbitrary waveforms. The idea is to create a waveform of an arbitrary shape; not just the usual sines, squares and triangles (although that's possible, too). Arbitrary waveforms can be realized using analog oscillator techniques coupled with wave shaping circuits but it can be a challenge to do well. Instead, consider creating a large table of integer values. Typically, the table size would be a nice power of two, like 256. Each entry in the table would be the digitized value of the desired waveform. A simple ramp might look like this:

```
unsigned short int ramp_table[] = { 0, 1, 2, 3, /* and so on */};
```

A more complicated wave might look like this:

```
unsigned short int squiggly_table[] = { 0, 21, 15, 33, /* etc */};
```

These values could then be sent sequentially to a digital-to-analog converter (DAC) to create the desired waveform. Once we get to the end of the table, we simply loop back to the start to make the next cycle. With a 256 entry table, we can use an `unsigned char` as the table index and once it reaches 255, incrementing it will cause it to roll over back to 0, automatically. The post increment operator is ideal for this. For the code below, assume PORT is the memory location of the DAC we are writing to.

```
unsigned char i = 0;

// loop forever
while ( 1 )
{
    PORT = ramp_table[i++];

    // now wait between each value, dependent on sample rate
    delay();
}
```

9.4 Error Correction via Table Translation

Another possible use for a look-up table is for error correction. Again, let's limit this to a nice 256 entry table. Suppose you are reading a sensor with an 8 bit (256 level) analog-to-digital converter (ADC). Maybe this is a temperature sensor and at the extremes of the temperature range it tends to go out of calibration. You can use the input value from the sensor (perhaps appropriately scaled and then turned into an integer) as the index into a 256 element table that contains the corrected values.

As an example, to keep it simple let's say the sensor reads a temperature ranging from 0 °C to 250°C. You calibrate it by placing it in a known 150°C oven and the sensor reads 145° instead of the ideal 150°. You repeat this process at several other temperatures and discover that it reads 166° when it's really 170°, 188° when it's really 195°, and so on. So you create a table where the 145th entry is 150, the 166th entry is 170, the 188th entry is 195, etc. Now use the sensor value as the index into the array. The value you access is the corrected result. The table effectively translates your input into a calibrated output.

```
corrected_temp = calibration_array[ sensor_value ];
```

This is a very fast process and as accurate as your calibration measurements. As long as the sensor data is repeatable (e.g., it always reads 145°C in a 150°C oven), you'll get good results.

10. C Structures

10.1 Introduction

C allows compound data called structures, or `struct` for short. The idea is to use a variety of the basic data types such as `float` or `int` to describe some sort of object. Structures may contain several of each type along with pointers, arrays, and even other structures. There are many uses for such a construct and structures are very common in production C code.

As an example, we may wish to describe an electronic component such as a transistor. What sort of things do we need? There are several performance parameters that may be used such as current gain, breakdown voltage and maximum power dissipation. All of these items may be represented as `double` variables. There will be a model number. This will probably be a string as it may contain letters (such as "2N3904"). There will need to be a manufacturer's code. This could be an `int`. A real world device will have many more parameters than these five, but these will suffice for our purposes. If you only have one transistor to deal with, five separate variables is not a big deal to keep track of. On the other hand, what if you have a great number of parts as in a database? Perhaps there are 1000 devices. Creating 5000 separate variables and keeping them straight presents a bit of a challenge. It would be nice if we could combine the five items together into a "super variable". Then, all we have to worry about is creating 1000 of them for the database (perhaps with an array, although there are other techniques). There shouldn't be a problem of getting the current gain of one device confused with that of another. This is where structures come in. Below is an example of how we would define this transistor structure and associated instances.

```
struct transistor {
        double      currentgain;
        double      breakdown;
        double      maxpower;
        short int   manufacturer;
        char        model[20];
};

struct transistor my_transistor;
struct transistor *ptransistor;
```

We have defined a structure of type `transistor`. We have also declared an instance of a `struct transistor` called *my_transistor*, along with a pointer to a `struct transistor` called *ptransistor*. The five elements are referred to as the *fields* of the structure (e.g., the `currentgain` field). Note that this structure contains an array of characters for the model name/number. The model cannot exceed 19 characters (19 plus terminating null yields 20 declared). It is unlikely that we'll ever have model name/number this long, but if by chance we do, we will have to truncate it.

To set or retrieve values from an instance, we use a period to separate the structure name from the field of interest. Here are some examples:

```
my_transistor.currentgain = 200.0;
my_transistor.maxpower = 50.0;
my_transistor.manufacturer = 23;
```

In the last assignment, it may be better to use a `#define` rather than a hard number. For example, place the following definition in a header file and then use the assignment below:

```
#define MOTOROLA 23

my_transistor.manufacturer = MOTOROLA;
```

To set the model field, you could do something like this:

```
strcpy( my_transistor.model, "2N3904" );
```

Remember, `strcpy()` needs addresses. The double quote string literal produces this automatically. For the model field, we are using the shortcut described in earlier work. The line above is equivalent to:

```
strcpy( &(my_transistor.model[0]), "2N3904" );
```

If you need to use a field in a computation or comparison, the access is unchanged:

```
if( my_transistor.breakdown > 75.0 )
    printf("Breakdown voltage is at least 75 volts!\n");
```

A good question at this point is whether of not the declared order of the fields makes any difference. This depends on the compiler and target hardware. In some processors, multiple-byte variables such as long and short integers, floats and pointers must be *word aligned*. For example, a short int may be required to start on an even address or a float might be required to start on an address divisible by four. In such a system, a structure declared with the order of char, float, char, int will need *pad bytes* between some fields to ensure alignment and will take up more memory space than if the structure was organized as float, int, char, char. This is of particular importance if large arrays of structures are to be used.

10.2 Pointers and Structures

It is generally not a good practice to send entire structures to functions as arguments. The reason is because you wind up copying a lot of data. The transistor structure above contains three `doubles` at 8 bytes each, a `short int` at 2 bytes, and 20 bytes for the `char` array, leaving a total of 46 bytes of memory that need to be copied if we pass this to a function. It would be much more efficient if we simply passed the starting address of the structure to the function. That is, we tell the function where to find the structure by using a pointer (this is called "passing by reference" versus the more familiar "passing by value"). This is why we declared `ptransistor`. We initialize it like so:

```
ptransistor = &my_transistor;
```

To access the various fields, we can longer use the period because we no longer have a `struct transistor`; we have a pointer to one. For pointers, we access the fields via the pointer token, which is made up of a dash followed by a greater than sign: -> Thus, we might say:

```
ptransistor->currentgain = 200.0;
strcpy( ptransistor->model, "2N3904" );
```

Embedded Controllers

Below is a function that simply prints out the values of the various fields.

```
void print_transistor( struct transistor *pt )
{
      printf("For model: %s\n", pt->model );
      printf("Current gain is %lf\n", pt->currentgain );
      printf("Breakdown voltage is %lf\n", pt->breakdown );
      printf("Maximum power is %lf\n", pt->maxpower );
}
/* note use of %s for string and %lf for "long float" i.e., double */
```

We pass the function a pointer to a transistor structure like so:

```
print_transistor( &my_transistor );

/* we could also use print_transistor( ptransistor );
   if we initialized it as above */
```

10.3 Structures, Arrays, and So On

We have seen that it is possible to have arrays within structures. It is also possible to have structures within structures and pointers within structures. Here are some examples:

```
/* The structure definitions */
struct foo {
      float x;
      float y;
};

struct bar {
      double *pd;
      struct foo littlefoo;
      struct foo *pf;
};

/* The variable declarations */
struct foo my_foo;
struct bar my_bar;
struct bar *pbar = &my_bar;
double z=1.0;
```

The `bar` structure contains a pointer to a `double`, a pointer to `struct foo`, and a `struct foo`. We would access them as follows:

```
my_bar.pd = &z; /* pd isn't a double but the address of one, hence & */
my_bar.littlefoo.x = 2.2;
pbar->littlefoo.y = 3.3;
pbar->pf = &my_foo;
pbar->pf->x = 4.4;
```

Note that if you didn't say `pbar->pf = &my_foo;` first, then `pbar->pf->x = 4.4;` would be very evil! Without assigning `my_foo` to `pf`, this pointer would contain some random number. The second statement would then use that number as the starting address of `struct foo`, and write the number 4.4 where the x field should be. As it's highly unlikely that this random number is the starting address of a `struct foo`, the number 4.4 overwrites something else. That might mean other data or even code gets destroyed. Your program behaves erratically or crashes.

Pointer Rule Number One: Never dereference[8] an uninitialized pointer!

Only bad, evil things will happen and you will become a very sad programmer.

At the beginning of the transistor example we noted that we might want to create a bunch of transistors. One possibility is to use an array. There are other ways, as we shall see. Here's how you'd declare an array of 1000 transistor structures, given the definition above:

```
struct transistor transistors[1000];
```

You would access the field as follows:

```
transistors[0].currentgain = 200.0; /* set 1st device's gain to 200 */
transistors[2].breakdown = 85.0;    /* set 3rd device's breakdown to 85 */
```

Finally, it is also possible to create an array of pointers to transistor structures:

```
struct transistor *ptarray[1000];
```

Note that we do not have 1000 transistor structures, but rather 1000 pointers. Each of these would need to point to an appropriate transistor structure. Assuming you had declared one named `my_transistor` as we did earlier, you could write:

```
ptarray[0] = &my_transistor;
```

And you could access fields like so:

```
ptarray[0]->maxpower = 25.0;
```

Although this may look a little odd at first, this sort of construct does have some good uses in more advanced applications. To stretch your mind just a teensy bit further, C makes it possible to create something like an array of pointers to structures which contain a structure which in turn contains an array of pointers to still other structures. Read that again, imagine what that might look like as a memory map, and then write some possible definitions/declarations. If you can do that, you've pretty well mastered the idea.

10.4 Exercises

1. Declare a structure of type `Quest` called `Grail` that contains a float called `X`, a long integer called `Y` and an unsigned character called `Z`.

2. Given the structure of problem one, will the order of the three fields have any effect or importance? How might we determine if it does?

---

[8] i.e., try to access the fields of.

11. C Linked Lists

11.1 Introduction

A linked list is an alternate way to collect together a number of instances of a given data type. Compared to arrays, linked lists offer the advantages of not requiring contiguous memory for the collection and an easy way to re-order the collection by simply swapping pointers. As we shall see later, linked lists are also very flexible when it comes to adding or deleting items to the collection. On the downside, linked lists require somewhat more memory than arrays (since space for pointers must be included), and arrays offer consistent fast access to any member of the array (linked lists require that the list be "walked along" in order to get to a given member). To create a linked list, a pointer to the structure type is included in the definition of the structure. Once the instances of the structure type are created, they are strung together by placing appropriate addresses in the pointer field.

A graphical example is shown below with four instances of some structure:

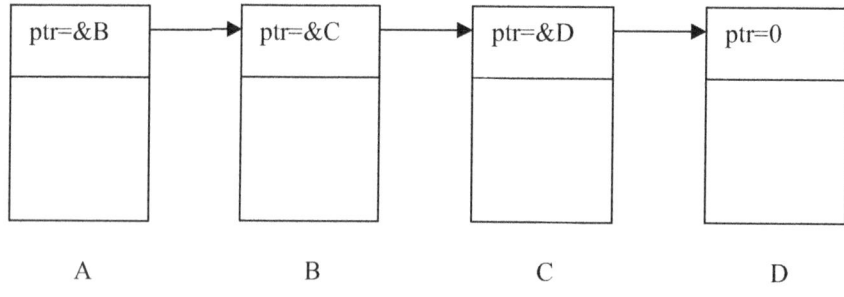

Figure 11.1, linked list

Imagine that each structure is 100 bytes in size. Further, assume that A is located at memory address 1000 (spanning 1000 to 1099), B is a located at address 2000, C at 3000, and D at 4000. Each structure contains a pointer to the next one in the list. A contains a pointer to the address of B, B to C, and so forth. For example, the value of A's pointer is 2000 (the memory address of B), while the value of C's pointer is 4000 (the address of D).

Note that &A is the top of the list, and that the last item signifies that no items remain by having its pointer set to 0. Further, these four items could be linked in any manner by simply changing the pointer values. Finally, items A, B, C, and D may reside anywhere in the memory map; they need not be contiguous. In contrast, if we were to make an array out of these structures, they would need to be packed into memory in sequence in order to be indexed properly. That is, if A were located at address 1000, B would have to be at 1100, C at 1200, and D at 1300, as they are each 100 bytes in size[9]. If you wanted to rearrange the structures (e.g., to sort them), add new ones or delete existing ones, this would require quite a bit of work

---

[9] Array indexing works by simply multiplying the index value by the size of the arrayed item, and then using this value as an offset from the starting address. Thus, in this example, item[2] (i.e., C) is found by multiplying the index of 2 by the size of 100 bytes to achieve a 200 offset from the starting location of address 1000, or 1200. Remember, item[0] is A, while item[1] is B, and item[2] is C.

with an array. These tasks are much easier with a linked list because the structures themselves aren't manipulated, only the associated pointers.

11.2 Linked List Example

Now for a concrete example. A typical structure definition may look something like this:

```
struct Marmot {
      struct Marmot *NextMarmot;
      float Age;
      float Weight;
};
```

We could declare three instances of Marmots and link them together as follows:

```
struct Marmot Larry = { 0, 3.4,  19.7 };
struct Marmot Jane = { &Larry, 2.5, 13.1 };
struct Marmot Felix = { &Jane, 2.9, 15.6 };
```

`Felix` is at the top of the list, while `Larry` is at the bottom. Note that the items must be declared in inverse order since the pointer reference must exist prior to assignment (i.e., `Jane` must exist in order for `Felix` to use `Jane`'s address). It is common to also declare a pointer to use as the head of the list. Thus, we might also add:

```
struct Marmot *MarmotList = &Felix;
```

Thus, the following are true:

```
Felix.NextMarmot points to Jane
MarmotList->NextMarmot points to Jane
Jane.NextMarmot points to Larry
MarmotList->NextMarmot->NextMarmot points to Larry
Larry.NextMarmot is 0
MarmotList->NextMarmot->NextMarmot->NextMarmot is 0
```

The final line of pointers to pointers is not very practical. To get around this, we can use a temporary pointer. Below is an example function that takes the head of a `Marmot` list as its argument, and then prints out the ages of all of the `Marmot`s in the list.

```
void PrintMarmotAges( struct Marmot *top )
{
      struct Marmot *temp;

      temp = top; /* initialize pointer to top of list */

      while( temp ) /* true only if marmot exists */
      {
            printf( "%f\n", temp->Age );
            temp = temp->NextMarmot );
      }
}
```

It would be called like so:

```
PrintMarmotAges( MarmotList );
```

Note that we could've reused `top` rather than use the local `temp` in this case. If the head of the list will be needed for something else in the function though, then the local variable will be required (i.e., since `temp = temp->NextMarmot` effectively erases the prior value of `temp`, we lose the head of the list as we walk down the list).

11.3 Exercise

A bipolar transistor can be described (partially) with the following information: A part number (such as "2N3904"), a typical beta, and maximum ratings for P_d, I_c, and BV_{ceo}. Using the data below, create a program that would allow the user to search for devices that meet a minimum specified requirement for beta, P_d, I_c, or BV_{ceo}. Devices that meet the performance spec would be printed out in a table (all data fields shown). If no devices meet the spec, an appropriate message should be printed instead. For example, a user could search for devices that have a P_d of at least 25 watts. All devices with $P_d >= 25.0$ would be printed out.

```
Device      Beta        Pd(W)       Ic(A)       BVceo(V)

2N3904      150         .35         .2          40
2N2202      120         .5          .3          35
2N3055      60          120         10          90
2N1013      95          50          4           110
MPE106      140         15          1.5         35
MC1301      80          10          .9          200
ECG1201     130         1.3         1.1         55
```

12. C Memory

12.1 Introduction

Up until now, whenever we have needed variables we simply declared them, either globally or locally. There are times, however, when this approach is not practical. Consider a program that must deal with a large amount of data from external files such as a word processor, or graphics or sound editor. In all instances the application may need to open very large files, sometimes many megabytes in size. The issue is not merely the size. After all, you could declare a very large array, or perhaps several of them. The problem is that the data is both large and variable in size. For example, you might edit a sound file that's 100k bytes in size, but you might also need to edit one that's 100 times larger. It would not be wise to declare a 10 megabyte array when you only need 100k. Further, you can guarantee that if you do declare 10 megabytes, the day will come when you'll need 11 megabytes. What is needed is some way of dynamically allocating memory of the size needed, when needed.

12.2 Free Memory Pool

In a given computer, memory is used by the operating system as well as by any running applications. Any memory left over is considered to be part of the "free memory pool". This pool is not necessarily contiguous. It may be broken up into several different sized chunks. It all depends on the applications being run and how the operating system deals with them. The total amount of free memory and the locations of the various chunks will change over time. C offers ways of "asking" the operating system for a block of memory from the free pool. If the operating system can grant your request, you will have access to the memory and can use it as you see fit. When you are through using the memory, you tell the operating system that you are done with it so that it can reuse it elsewhere. Sounds simple, right? Well, it is!

12.3 Allocating Memory

To use the memory routines, include the `stdlib.h` header in your code and be sure to link with the standard library. There are two main memory allocation functions. They are `malloc()` and `calloc()`. Here are their prototypes:

```
void * malloc( unsigned int size );
void * calloc( unsigned int num_item, unsigned int item_size );
```

`malloc()` takes a single argument: The number of bytes that you wish to allocate from the free pool. `calloc()` takes two arguments: The number of items that you want to fit into the memory block and their size in bytes. Basically, `calloc()` just calls `malloc()` after multiplying the two arguments together. It is used for convenience. Both functions return a pointer to a type `void`. What is this? A `void` pointer can be thought of as a generic, one-size-fits-all pointer. It prevents possible type size clashes. You can assign a `void` pointer to another type of pointer and not get a type mismatch. If the memory request cannot be made (not enough memory) then the functions will return `NULL`. **Always check for the `NULL` return! Never assume that the allocation will work!**

If you want to obtain space for 100 bytes, you'd do something like this:

```
char *cp;

cp = malloc( 100 );
if( cp )
{
      /* memory allocated, do stuff... */
}
else
{
      /* not allocated, warn user and fail gracefully... */
}
```

If you need space for 200 `doubles`, you'd do something like this:

```
double *dp;

if( dp = calloc( 200, sizeof(double) ) )   /* assign and if test in 1 */
{
      /* memory allocated, do stuff... */
}
else
{
      /* not allocated, warn user and fail gracefully... */
}
```

Note the use of the `sizeof()` operator above. If you had a structure and needed to create one (for example, to add to a linked list), you might do this:

```
struct foo *fp;

if( fp = calloc( 1, sizeof(struct foo) ) )
{
      /* remainder as above ... */
```

12.4 Using Memory

The pointer that is returned from the allocation function is used as the base of the object or array of objects in which you're interested. Keeping it simple, suppose you want to allocate an array of three integers. If you want to set the first element to 0, and the second and third elements to 1, do the following (code fragment only, error processing not shown):

```
int *ip;

if( ip = calloc( 3, sizeof(int) ) )
{
      *ip = 0;
      *(ip+1) = 1;        /* could also say ip[1] = 1; */
      *(ip+2) = 1;        /* could also say ip[2] = 1; */
}
```

Embedded Controllers

Note the freedom that we have with the pointer. It can be used as a normal pointer or thought of as the base of an array and indexed accordingly. Similarly, we might need to allocate a structure and initialize its fields. Here is a function that we can call to allocate a `struct foobar`, initialize some fields, and return a pointer to it.

```c
struct foobar {
      double d;
      int i;
      char name[20];
};

/* other code... */

struct foobar * alloc_foobar( void )
{
      struct foobar *fp;

      if( fp = malloc( sizeof(struct foobar) ) )
      {
            fp->d = 12.0;     /* just some stuff to show how... */
            fp->i = 17;
            strcpy( fp->name, "Timmy" );
      }
      return( fp );
}
```

12.5 Freeing Memory

Once you're done using memory, you must return it to the free memory pool. If you don't, no other application (nor the operating system) can use it. The memory will be effectively lost until the system is rebooted. This is known as a memory leak. To return memory that you have no further use for, use `free()`. Here is the prototype:

```c
int free( void *p );
```

p is the pointer that you initially received from either `malloc()` or `calloc()`. The return value of the `free()` function is 0 for success or −1 on error. Normally this function never fails if it is given a valid pointer. If it does fail, there is little that you can do about it (at least not at this level). **Remember: Every block that you allocate eventually must be freed!** You might wonder why the `free()` function does not need to know the size of the block to free. This is because along with the memory they pass to you, `malloc()` and `calloc()` actually allocate a little bit more for use by the operating system. In this extra memory that you don't see are stored items such as the size of the block. This saves you a little house keeping work.

12.6 Operating System Specific Routines

Often the standard routines examined above are augmented with special routines unique to a given operating system. These might give you control over using virtual memory, presetting memory values, or allow you to obtain access to special kinds of memory (e.g., graphics memory).

12.7 Exercises

1. Write the code to allocate 1000 bytes of memory.

2. Write the code to allocate space for an array of 500 single precision floating point values.

3. Write the code to free the memory allocated in problems one and two.

13. C File IO

13.1 Introduction

High level fileio in C uses functions such as `fopen()`, `fclose()`, `fread()`, `fwrite`, `fprintf()`, `fgetc()`, and so on. These utilize a variable of type `FILE` to access disk files. They allow you to read and write data from/to files on disk in a manner very similar to sending data to the computer screen via `printf()` or retrieving data from the keyboard via `scanf()`.

Closer to home, we have low level fileio. These use a file descriptor, which is basically just an integer. High level functions actually call the low level functions anyway. There are five things you need to do with files. First, you open them to obtain access to an existing file or to create a new one. Next, you read or write data from/to the file. You may also need to move around in a file, perhaps to reread data or to skip over data. Finally, when you are finished using the file, you must close it. To open a file use:

```
fh = open( name, mode );
```

where

```
char *name: /* disk name of file */
int fh:     /* file descriptor */
int mode;   /* a define */
```

`fh` is the file descriptor that is needed for subsequent read/write calls. It will be `>= 0` if all is OK, `-1` on error.

Example modes:

   O_RDONLY   read only
   O_WRONLY   write only
   O_CREAT   create if not exists

To read/write data, use:

```
count = read( fh, buffer, len );
count = write( fh, buffer, len );
```

`fh` is the file descriptor returned from `open()`, `buffer` is the address of where to find/place data (i.e., the thing you're copying to disk or making a copy of from disk), `len` is the number of bytes to read/write, `count` is the actual number of bytes read/written.

A common construct is:

```
if( (count = read( fh, buf, len )) != len )
{
        //...there was an error, process it...
}
```

You can also skip around in a file:

```
apos = lseek( fh, rpos, mode );
```

where

```
long apos:    absolute position (-1 on error)
long rpos:    relative position
mode:         0 for relative to beginning of file (rpos >= 0)
              1 for relative to current position
              2 for relative to the end (rpos <= 0)
```

Note that your present position is `= lseek( fh, 0, 1 );`

When you are done with the file, you must close it:

```
error = close( fh );
```

`error` is `0` if all went OK, `-1` otherwise.

C allows you to have multiple files open simultaneously for reading and writing. You will need one file descriptor for each file open at the same time (they can be reused later, if desired).

Below is a program that can be used to investigate the contents of almost any kind of file. It uses a variety of techniques that we have examined through the course. Some lines have wrapped.

```c
/*              headdump.c

   This program spits out the first 128 bytes of a file in hex, decimal, and
   string form (non printable chars are printed out as periods). */

#include <stdio.h>
#include <stdlib.h>
#include <string.h>
#include <ctype.h>

#define CHUNKSIZE 128

unsigned char buf[CHUNKSIZE];

char *szerrmsgs[] = {
   "No errors on %s\n",
   "USAGE: %s <filename>\n",
   "Could not open %s\n",
   "Seek error on %s\n",
   "Position error on %s\n",
   "Rewind error on %s\n",
   "Read error on %s\n"
   };

void my_exit( FILE *fp, int err, char *pc )
{
   if( fp )    fclose( fp );
   if( err )   printf( szerrmsgs[err], pc ); /* don't bother if all OK */
   exit( err );
}
```

```c
void main( int argc, char *argv[] )
{
   int    size, c=0, x;
   FILE   *fp=0;

   if( (argc < 2) || ( !strcmp(argv[1], "?") ) )
      my_exit( fp, 1, argv[0] );

   if( fp = fopen( argv[1], "r" ) )
   {
      /* Find out how big the file is. If it's < CHUNKSIZE then read in
         what's available */
      if( -1 != fseek( fp, 0, 2 ) )    /* seek to end */
      {
         if( -1 != (size = ftell( fp )) )
         {
            if( size > CHUNKSIZE )  size = CHUNKSIZE;
            if( -1 != fseek( fp, 0, 0 ) )    /* seek to start */
            {
               if( fread( buf, 1, size, fp ) == (unsigned int)size )
               {
                  /* print this out as 8 chars by 16 (or so) lines, first hex,
                     then decimal, then string */
                  while( c < size )
                  {
                     /* print out line as hex */
                     printf("%3d: %02x%02x %02x%02x %02x%02x %02x%02x ",
c,buf[c],buf[c+1],buf[c+2],buf[c+3],buf[c+4],buf[c+5],buf[c+6],buf[c+7] );

                     /* print out line as decimal */
                     printf("   %03d%03d %03d%03d %03d%03d %03d%03d ",
buf[c],buf[c+1],buf[c+2],buf[c+3],buf[c+4],buf[c+5],buf[c+6],buf[c+7] );

                     /* print out line as string. check the chars and if not
                        printable, replace with periods */
                     for( x=0; x<8; x++ )
                     {
                        if( !isprint( buf[c+x] ) )
                           buf[c+x] = '.';
                     }
                     printf("   %c%c%c%c%c%c%c%c\n",buf[c],buf[c+1],buf[c+2],
buf[c+3],buf[c+4],buf[c+5],buf[c+6], buf[c+7] );

                     c+=8;
                  }
               }
               else
                  my_exit( fp, 6, argv[0] );
            }
            else
               my_exit( fp, 5, argv[0] );
         }
         else
            my_exit( fp, 4, argv[0] );
      }
      else
         my_exit( fp, 3, argv[0] );
   }
   else
      my_exit( fp, 2, argv[1] );

   my_exit( fp, 0, argv[1] );
}
```

14. C Command Line Args and More

14.1 Command Line Arguments

Question: How do various utilities "read" the arguments that you place after them on the command line? For example, you might have a utility that archives (compresses) a file, creating a new (compressed) file. You might use it like this from a DOS or shell prompt:

```
C:>archive foo.txt foo.arc
```

The program is called `archive` (archive.exe), and you're telling it to compress the file `foo.txt` and create a new file called `foo.arc`. This is much faster than using `scanf()` type input from within the program (i.e., having the user run the program, at which point the program then prompts for the two file names). C allows a very simple method of obtaining these command line arguments. This requires a modification to the declaration of `main()`:

```
void main( int argc, char *argv[] )
```

The first parameter is called the argument count and tells you how many items (strings) where entered on the command line. In the example above, `argc` would be 3. The second parameter is called the argument vector. It is an array of pointers to strings. These strings are the items entered on the command line. Thus `argv[0]` points to "archive", `argv[1]` points to "foo.txt", and `argv[2]` points to "foo.arc".

If `argc` is 1, then no arguments were added after the executable name. Below is a simple echo example. This will echo whatever was typed in on the command line.

```
void main( int argc, char *argv[] )
{
        int x;

        for( x=0; x<argc; x++ )
                printf( "Argument %d is %s\n", x, argv[x] );
}
```

Note that since `argv` is an array of pointers, then `argv[x]` is also a pointer, and is treated just like any other pointer to characters. Thus, you can use functions like `strcpy()` or `strcmp()` on it. For numeric arguments (such as "archive blah 23"), you may convert the ASCII string ("23") into either an integer, long integer, or float via the `atoi()`, `atol()`, and `atof()` functions, respectively.

Other possibilities include printing out directions if `argc` is 1 or if the only added argument is "?". It is possible to take this further by adding "switches" or "flags" to the argument list so that arguments can be presented in any order. This is precisely what is done if the compiler or linker is run directly rather than via the IDE.

In summation, command line arguments are a very handy and quick way of getting values into a program. As an exercise, alter one of your previous programs to utilize command line arguments rather than the `scanf()` approach.

14.2 Conditional Compilation

Suppose for a moment that you wish to create two or more versions of a program that differ only in mild ways. While it is possible to maintain multiple sets of source code for each, this can be a pain when it comes time to fix a bug or add a feature since alterations will need to be made to each of the source files. It would be much easier to somehow "flag" parts of the source code as belonging to different versions of the program and then have the compiler or preprocessor do the work for you. This is exactly what conditional compilation is. To do this, we exploit the power of the preprocessor. We have already looked at the `#define` directive as a way of defining constants or creating macros, but we can take it further. Look at the following example fragment:

```
#define VERSION_A

#ifdef VERSION_A
char title[] = "This is version A";
#else
char title[] = "This is some other version";
#endif
```

The `#if`/`#else`/`#endif` directives act similarly to the `if`/`else` commands. Note that parentheses are not used to block multi-line sections (hence the need for the `#endif` directive). In the example above, the `char` array title is initialized to `"This is version A"`. If we commented out the `#define VERSION_A` line, then `title` would be initialized to `"This is some other version"`. In some IDEs it is possible to create variations on projects. Within each project you can define certain symbols (such as `VERSION_A`). This way you wouldn't even have to comment/uncomment the `#define`, but just select the desired project variation. Note that it is possible to nest `#if`/`else` directives. Further, you are not limited to simply altering global declarations. This technique can be used on code as well as data. In fact, entire functions may be added or excluded in this way. Here is another typical use:

```
void some_func( void )
{
        //...code stuff...

#ifdef DEBUG
    printf("Error in some_func, x=%d\n", x );
#endif

//...rest of function...
}
```

If `DEBUG` is defined, the `printf()` call will be included in the executable. If it is not defined, it is as if the `printf()` call never existed.

14.3 Exercise

Add `DEBUG printf()` statements to any of your existing programs. Compile with and without the `DEBUG` directive.

15. Embedded Programming

15.1 Introduction

As mentioned earlier, it is possible to break down computer programming into two broad camps: desktop applications and embedded applications. The embedded application market is ubiquitous but somewhat hidden to the average user. A typical person doesn't even realize that they're running an embedded program while they're using their cell phone, DVD player or microwave oven. Certainly, the trappings of a "normal" computer generally do not exist in these instances; there's usually no monitor or keyboard to speak of. From a programmer's perspective, what's different about the two and how is program development and testing affected?

15.2 Input/Output

Consider a typical embedded application such as a programmable or "intelligent" thermostat. Unlike a normal electro-mechanical thermostat, these devices allow the home owner to automatically change temperature at different times of the day in order to save energy. After all, why have the heat or air conditioner running when no one's home? Certainly, these devices do not come with a monitor or keyboard. In their place may be a small LCD display with a few fixed messages and a two digit numeric display for the temperature. For input there may be as few as two or three buttons for programming (set item plus up and down). By comparison, a microwave oven will probably have a complete numeric keypad with a series of special function buttons along with multiple seven-segment displays, or possibly several alpha-numeric displays for short messages. In any case, these devices are far different from the standard desktop computer. Consequently, a programmer's approach to input and output processing will be much different in the embedded case.

To start with, it is unlikely that there will be `printf()` and `scanf()` style functions. They are largely worthless in this world. What use would `printf()` be if all you have for output hardware is a bunch of LEDs? For input, you often need to read the state of switches, pushbuttons, and possibly some form of level control such as a rotary knob. For output, you often need to simply light an LED or set a value on a seven-segment display. For "fixed" style messages, these also need only a single signal to turn them on or off, such as an LED. In more advanced applications, a multi-line alphanumeric display may be available so setting individual letters is a possibility. In almost all cases these chores are handled by setting or clearing bits on specific output or inputs ports on the microcontroller. Some ports may be set up as a byte or word. Further, some ports may be bi-directional, meaning that they can behave as either input or output depending on some other register setting. Ports are little more than pins on the microcontroller that are hooked up to external circuitry. Thus, if a port is connected to an LED circuit, setting the output of the port HIGH could light the LED while setting the port LOW could turn off the LED. The obvious question then is "How do you read from or write to a port?" In many cases ports will be *memory mapped*. That is, a specific address in the memory map is allocated to a given port. You read and write from/to it just like any other variable. Further, development systems sometimes disguise these addresses as pre-defined global variables. They might also include a library of specific routines to utilize the ports. Thus setting a certain port (let's call it the "A" port) to a high might be as simple as `PORT_A = 1;` or `set_portA(1);`. Reading from a port might be something like `a = PORT_A;` or `a = get_portA();`. Consequently, embedded code is often all about reading and writing to/from ports and then branching to the requested chores.

There are some tricks to this. For example, how do you know if a key has been pressed? Calling `get_portA()` tells you the state of the switch connected to port A at the instant you call it. There is no "history" here if this is a simple momentary pushbutton instead of a toggle switch. In a case like this you might "poll" the port waiting for something to happen. This involves using a simple loop and repeatedly reading the port state in the loop. The code breaks out when the state changes:

```
while( get_portA() );
```

This will keep looping until `get_portA()` returns 0. Of course if you need to monitor several ports as is typical, you'll need to read a value from each for the test. This form of monitoring while waiting for something to happen is called an *event loop*. It may not be evident, but your house and car are probably filled with devices running event loops, just waiting for you to do something! These loops execute fairly fast so a time lag between your push and the resulting action is not noticed. On the output end, a port normally stays at the value you set it, so there is no need for a loop to "keep it set".

For more complicated displays such as a seven segment or alpha-numeric device, you may need to create a table of values indicating bit patterns for each numeral or letter to be displayed. These patterns, or words, would then be sent out various ports that are in turn connected to the displays.

For variable input devices such as a volume control, the external device (knob, slider, sensor, etc.) will be connected to an *analog to digital converter* or ADC. This might be a separate circuit or the controller may have these built-in. The converter turns the analog voltage into a numeric value that you can read from a port. For example, a volume control may be just a potentiometer connected to a fixed voltage. As the knob is moved, the voltage at the wiper arm will change. The A/D converter may encode this into a single byte. A byte ranges from 0 to 255 in value. Thus, if the volume is at maximum, the port will read 255. If the volume is at halfway the port will read about 127, and finally 0 when the volume is off.

15.3 Math

Usually, embedded code is not math intensive. There are some exceptions to this rule, but generally code for a microwave oven doesn't need something like a cosine function. Many embedded systems do not have or need floating point math. All math operations are performed using integers. Look-up tables may be used to speed processing in some cases. You will sometimes hear of "fixed point" math versus floating point. This is a fairly simple idea. Suppose you need to work with variables to the precision of tenths but you only have integers. Simply treat your variables as having an unseen decimal point after the first digit and think of all values as being in tenths. Thus, the number 17.3 would be stored and manipulated as 173. If the result of some calculation is say, 2546, then you know the real answer is 254.6.

15.4 Memory and Hardware

Most embedded applications just run one piece of code. Therefore, you can think of a program as "owning" everything. There's no sharing of resources. This makes life easy in many regards. For example, there's not much need for an operating system. Also, the system is "known" in that your code will be running on fixed hardware. Execution times are very predictable. Of course, the computational power of the processors tends to be much less than in the desktop world. Still, you can do things that are not practical in the desktop world due to hardware variation. A classic example is a "timing loop". Sometimes you need to create a time delay or to "waste" a certain amount of time, perhaps for synchronization to some external hardware. You can do this with a simple loop that iterates a specific number of times:

```
for( c=0; c<1000; c++ );
```

This loop does nothing but count, but each count will require a certain number of clock cycles from the microcontroller, and thus a specific time. These are usually determined experimentally. You could sit down with the processor manuals and figure out how long a loop will take, but it's usually easier to just write the thing and try a few values. The result will depend on the specific microcontroller used as well as its clock frequency.

15.5 Code Development

The real "kicker" is that you can't do *native development* with embedded code. In other words, you can't program the microcontroller just using the microcontroller the way you can create desktop applications using a desktop computer. Instead, you need to have a *host* and a *target*. The host is the computer you use for development (such as a normal desktop unit) while the target is the thing you're developing for (the embedded application). The compiler that you use is technically referred to as a *cross-compiler* because it creates machine code for a processor other than the one the host uses. For example, your PC might use a Pentium processor, but the cross-compiler that runs on it creates machine code for a specific Atmel AVR microcontroller. To test your code, you need to either simulate the target on the host, or you can download the compiled code to the target and test it there. This is an extra, but unavoidable, step.

16. Hardware Architecture

16.1 Introduction

Arguably, the first commercial microprocessor was the Intel 4004 released in 1971. It was a four bit processor and was comprised of a series of ICs. A year later, Intel released the 8008, an eight bit processor on a single chip. The remainder of the decade saw the development of numerous microprocessor and microcontroller lines from various manufacturers including the 8088, Z80, 6502, 6809 and 68000 to name a few. These served as the core of the first generation of home computers. Their performance, while impressive for the day, pales in comparison with modern processors. Many used clock frequencies in the 1 to 5 MHz region and could access only modest amounts of memory (typically less than one megabyte). Integration of electronic control into everyday consumer items such as cars, microwave ovens and TVs, gained momentum during this time yielding the *microcontroller*. A microcontroller can be thought of as a specialized microprocessor. Typically, they do not have the computational power of microprocessors but instead feature other functional blocks that are useful when interfacing to sensors, actuators, display devices and the like that are found in consumer or industrial electronics.

While the design of any particular microcontroller will be unique, there are certain themes and elements that are consistent. Unlike a microprocessor used in a personal computer, a microcontroller is generally an all-in-one solution designed to reduce cost and save space. For example, the code and data space requirements for an embedded application tend to be quite small compared to traditional desktop applications. Consequently, all memory is included on the microcontroller (not to be confused with the *cache memory* found on microprocessors which exists primarily to increase the computational speed of the unit). Further, the microcontroller will include functional blocks such as independent programmable timers, general purpose digital input/output (GPIO) ports and analog input ports featuring ADCs with eight or more bits of resolution. Some controllers also contain digital to analog converters for direct analog signal generation or other specialized blocks for dealing with serial communications, wireless communications and so forth. As a microcontroller can have a large number of these interface blocks, it is not always cost effective to dedicate external IC pins for each and every input and output function. Consequently, pins are usually multiplexed, each offering multiple possible uses. For example, a specific pin might be programmed for digital input, digital output or a pulse-width modulated output (obviously, not simultaneously).

As mentioned in Chapter Two, processors might use a shared memory scheme for code and data (Von Neumann architecture) or a split memory scheme (Harvard architecture). Harvard architecture is somewhat less flexible but it allows for faster processing as the processor can fetch new instructions very quickly and without any collision with data access. In the case of microcontrollers, it is worth noting that the memory holding the code must be *non-volatile* otherwise the control program will cease to exist once power is cycled.

The other major item of importance in microprocessor/microcontroller architecture is the type of instruction set used. The two basic choices are CISC (Complex Instruction Set Computing) and RISC (Reduced Instruction Set Computing). A CISC processor contains instructions that might offer several low-level steps rolled into one. While this sounds very convenient, the down side is that these instructions often take several clock cycles to execute. By comparison, RISC architectures do not use these complex instructions, instead focusing on getting each instruction to execute in a single cycle. These are usually *pipelined* as well, meaning that while one instruction is executed, the next instruction is being loaded from program memory. RISC processors are used in everything from simple embedded applications to cell phones to supercomputers. Two examples of embedded RISC processors are the Atmel AVR and the ARM. These can be found in applications such as tablet devices, smart phones, game consoles, game controllers and automotive controllers. The AVR is the core of the ATmega processors used in most Arduino controller boards. We shall examine the Arduino system in the following chapters.

16.2 Atmel AVR Core

The Atmel AVR processor core uses Harvard architecture with simple pipelining. A block diagram of the AVR series core is shown below.

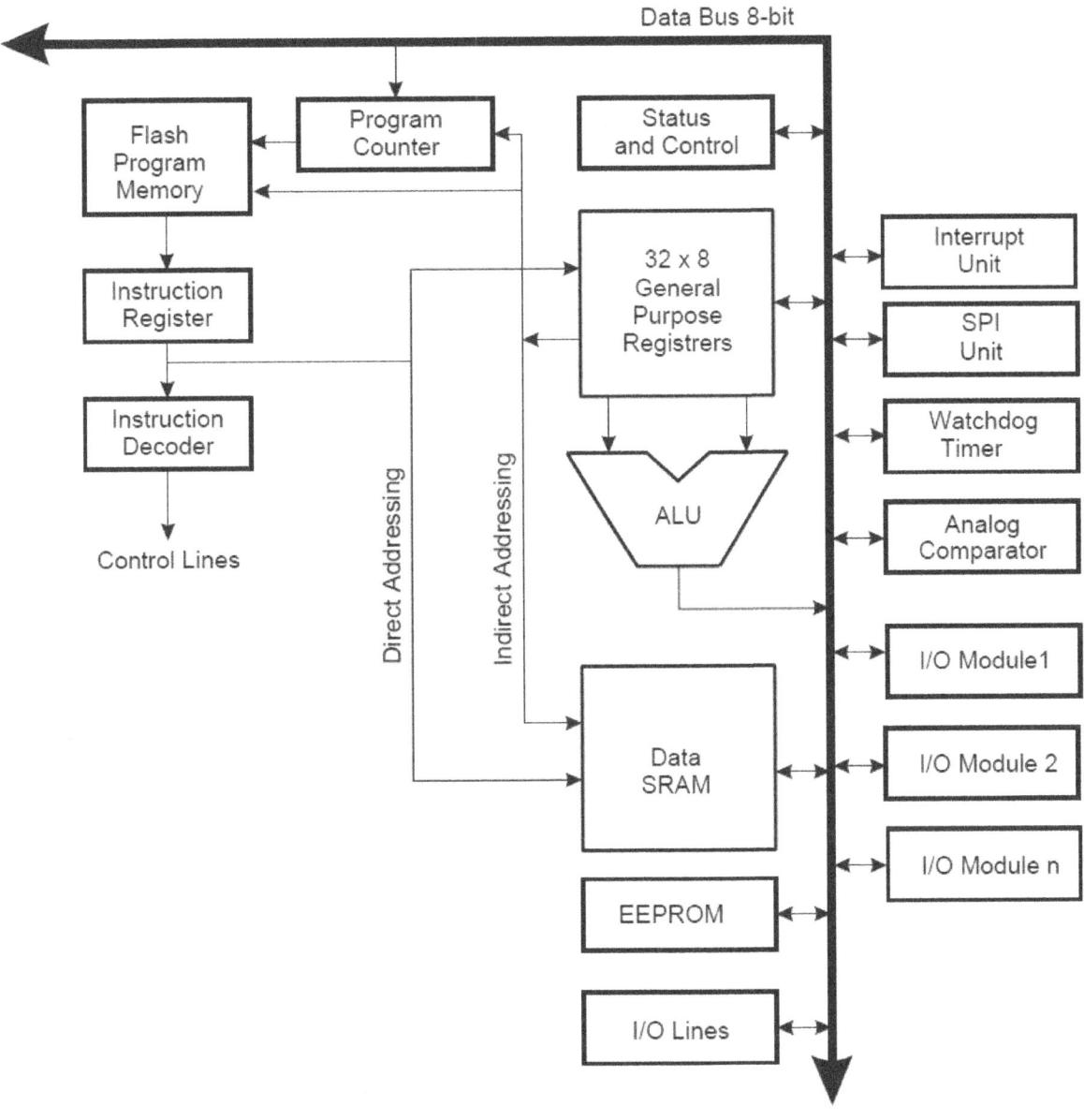

Figure 16.1, AVR block diagram (Atmel 2014)

Embedded Controllers

The first thing to notice is that most of the blocks are interconnected via an eight bit *data bus* (i.e., a collection of parallel connections, in this case, eight of them). The data bus is bidirectional meaning that data can be placed onto it (written) by one block and pulled off (read) by another. Obviously, some form of "traffic control" needs to be applied and that is usually handled by appropriate timing signals and tri-state buffers[10].

The ALU, or Arithmetic Logic Unit, is responsible for basic computational functions such as integer addition and subtraction, bit operations, comparisons and the like. In association with this are 32 eight bit general purpose registers. The ALU performs operations on the values in the registers, not directly on values in general memory. For example, suppose you want to add two variables and place the result in a third variable. The ALU has to transfer values from memory to the registers where the computation is performed and then transfer the result back to the final location. A large number of registers is a common feature of RISC processors. Early CISC processors had very few registers (indeed, many had a single "accumulator" for these sorts of operations). There are also many specialized registers not shown here as they are associated with IO modules, timers and so forth (more on this in a moment). Three important specialized registers are the *status register*, *program counter* and *stack pointer*. The program counter (PC) keeps track of the currently executing instruction (i.e., the current location of the code flow). The stack pointer (SP) records the current memory address of the top of the stack (i.e., the location in memory used for temporary variables and such). The status register (SR) contains a series of bits reflecting the most recent results of an ALU operation and the general state of the processor. The AVR status register contains eight bits, all of which are read/write and initialized at 0:

Bit	7	6	5	4	3	2	1	0
Function	I	T	H	S	V	N	Z	C

Figure 16.2, AVR status register (Atmel 2014)

The bits are as follows from the Atmel documentation:

Bit 7 – I: Global Interrupt Enable
The Global Interrupt Enable bit must be set for the interrupts to be enabled. The individual interrupt enable control is then performed in separate control registers. If the Global Interrupt Enable Register is cleared, none of the interrupts are enabled independent of the individual interrupt enable settings. The I-bit is cleared by hardware after an interrupt has occurred, and is set by the RETI instruction to enable subsequent interrupts. The I-bit can also be set and cleared by the application with the SEI and CLI instructions, as described in the instruction set reference.

Bit 6 – T: Bit Copy Storage
The Bit Copy instructions BLD (Bit LoaD) and BST (Bit STore) use the T-bit as source or destination for the operated bit. A bit from a register in the Register File can be copied into T by the BST instruction, and a bit in T can be copied into a bit in a register in the Register File by the BLD instruction.

Bit 5 – H: Half Carry Flag
The Half Carry Flag H indicates a Half Carry in some arithmetic operations. Half Carry Is useful in BCD arithmetic.

Bit 4 – S: Sign Bit, S = N $\oplus$ V
The S-bit is always an exclusive or between the Negative Flag N and the Two's Complement Overflow Flag V.

---

[10] A tri-state buffer simply repeats its input signal at its output like an ordinary buffer but also offers a third "high Z" state. When the high Z state is enabled, no output signal is present and the output impedance of the buffer goes to a very high value, effectively disconnecting the buffer from the bus.

> **Bit 3 – V: Two's Complement Overflow Flag**
> The Two's Complement Overflow Flag V supports two's complement arithmetic.
>
> **Bit 2 – N: Negative Flag**
> The Negative Flag N indicates a negative result in an arithmetic or logic operation.
>
> **Bit 1 – Z: Zero Flag**
> The Zero Flag Z indicates a zero result in an arithmetic or logic operation.
>
> **Bit 0 – C: Carry Flag**
> The Carry Flag C indicates a carry in an arithmetic or logic operation.

Figure 16.3, AVR status register bits (Atmel 2014)

It is important to remember that the state of the status register is not saved when entering an interrupt routine or restored when returning from an interrupt. This must be handled in software. We shall see how this is handled in future chapters.

16.3 Memory

Another important aspect is memory. Note that the AVR contains several different kinds of memory including flash program memory, static data memory or SRAM (Static Random Access Memory) and EEPROM (Electrically Erasable Programmable Read-Only Memory). Typical embedded applications run a single program repeatedly. This program must run from the moment the device is turned on until it is turned off. In many applications, this program is never updated (a microwave oven, perhaps). In other applications, it may be updated but only by qualified technicians, not by the consumer (for example, an automotive engine management system). Consequently, the program memory needs to be non-volatile, that is, it must be able to survive without power. Historically, this was done via ROM (Read-Only Memory) or PROM (Programmable Read-Only Memory). In both of these, individual bits can be set or cleared through the use of fuse/anti-fuse links. The difference is that ROMs are programmed at the time of manufacture while PROMs are programmed after manufacture. Both are permanent and cannot be reprogrammed. ROM is less expensive for large production runs but more expensive in small quantities. EEPROM has the advantage of being erasable and thus is a form of non-volatile read/write storage. Flash RAM is similar but is much less expensive. It has the downside that it must be programmed in blocks whereas EEPROM is byte-programmable. Therefore, Flash RAM (also called NVRAM) is ideal as a storage medium for the main program and EEPROM is useful as a medium for storing data that must survive a power cycle. A possible example use of EEPROM would involve saving user preference settings for a digital camera. When power is turned off and back on, the user expects the device to be "as they left it", not reverting back to a default state. Typically, special instructions or procedures are needed to write to or read from EEPROM.

In contrast to Flash RAM and EEPROM, SRAM is volatile, just like the common DRAM (Dynamic RAM) variants found in personal computers. Static RAM typically is made of six transistors arranged as a flip-flop for each bit of storage. DRAM, by comparison, typically consists of a single transistor-capacitor combination per bit. SRAM is less dense and more expensive per bit than DRAM but it is very fast and does not need to refreshed (the charge in a DRAM cell will leak over time requiring the cell to be refreshed at regular intervals). As a result, SRAM is used for general purpose registers and special purpose/IO registers. The ATmega 328P used in the Arduino Uno development board features 32k bytes of Flash RAM, 1k of EEPROM and 2k of SRAM. The Uno is detailed in the following chapter. By comparison, the ATmega 48A consists of 4k Flash, 256 bytes of EEPROM and 512 bytes of SRAM. Clearly, these are very modest memory footprints when compared to personal computers yet they are sufficient to power a wide range of applications. The 328P is by no means at the top of the heap, so to speak. Other controllers boast megabytes of addressable memory. There is, however, no need to over-specify a controller for a given embedded application. Extra memory that goes unused will not make the application faster; it will merely lead to more expensive hardware.

Continuing on, all of the registers in the AVR core are memory mapped, that is, they are tied to specific addresses in the SRAM. For example, the high (ADCH) and low (ADCL) bytes of the 328P's analog to digital converter output are found at addresses 0x79 and 0x78. Similarly, the output of port B (PORTB) is found at address 0x25 while the data direction register of port B (DDRB) is found at 0x24. A detailed table of all registers is found in the Atmel 2014 documentation under "Register Summary". A portion of these are available in the Appendix.

Finally, a series of other blocks such as the interrupt unit and the IO modules complete the design. We shall take a much closer look at these blocks in the upcoming chapters.

17. AVR ATmega 328P Overview

Or "Controlablanca: A Film Noir Microcontroller"[11]

"I need some assistance." Rick peered over the top of his work bench. It wasn't often that a dame walked into the lab, and a real looker at that. Beautiful, intelligent women had a way of turning his life into a burning hell and this one was a potential forest fire in heels. "Damn!" he cussed as he shook his finger, now blistering from its unfortunate collision with the hot soldering iron. Rick sidled up to her, somewhat wary. She was a knock-out, that's for sure; the kind of woman who could make Ingrid Bergman look bad on her best day and from her demeanor Rick assumed she was a grad from the polytechnical institute. Confident, tall and slender, she had the longest legs Rick had ever seen. "From her hips all the way down to the floor", as his companion, Frankie the lab rat, would say. What could she possibly want from his little lab? "What can I do you for, er, I mean, what can I do for you?" he stammered. "I've got a problem", she said in a voice so husky it could pull a dog sled. "I've got control issues and I need an expert." "Expert, eh? I think I know someone, Miss…Miss…What did you say your name was?" "I didn't", she responded. "It's Miss C." Rick furrowed his brow. "Missy? Missy who?" "Just Miss C", came her curt reply.

Rick looked over his shoulder at his lab partner. "Frankie, we're going down the hall to visit The Italian. Finish up the prototype but don't Bogart that 'scope 'cause Louie needs it." He turned to the dame, "Follow me", he said. They walked down the hall in silence until they came to a door with a small red, white and green flag sticker on it. Rick knocked. The door opened revealing a young man with dark hair and a five day old beard that was perfectly trimmed around the edges. Inside the office sat a large framed photo of a Ferrari, a few postcards from San Marino and what appeared to be spare parts for some manner of medieval coffee machine. "Si?" said the young man, one eyebrow raised, looking like a cross between a GQ model and Mr. Spock.

"Arduino, this is Missy", said Rick. "Che?" came the young man's response. "Not Kay, C", said the dame. Arduino looked at her and asked, "Not Casey, but who?" She sensed a possible language barrier and tried to meet him halfway. "Miss C, si?" she said. "Missy C", nodded Arduino. "No", she replied, her exasperation increasing, "Not CC, what am I, a compiler?" Arduino was getting confused now. "Nazi see what??" he asked, his eyes scanning up and down the hallway. The dame tried a different approach. "OK, suppose I was your mother's sister. I'd be aunt C", she countered. "Yeah, well if you was my mother's sister I'd be antsy, too", added Rick. The dame moved in close to Arduino and almost whispered through clenched teeth, "Look, just call me Miss C, see?" "Got it!" said Arduino. "Please come in. How can I help you Miss Seesi?" Rick shook his head as he lowered his gaze to the ground. How had the script devolved into a bad parody of an Abbott and Costello routine? Puns were more to his liking. Surely he'd have to Warn her Brothers about this. Of all the labs in all the colleges and universities in the world, why did she have to walk into his?

"What seems to be the problem, Miss Seesi?" asked Arduino. The dame was beginning to get a headache, the kind that builds from behind the eyes until it feels like your skull is filled with monkeys playing dodge ball. She took a deep breath and exhaled slowly. "I've got an application that's in trouble", she said. "*Trouble*," thought Rick, "yeah, I'll bet this dame knows all about *trouble*. It's part of the package with these ones, must be in their DNA. Why, if I was a bug she'd be a regular *Venus De Flytrap* – beautiful

---

[11] If you're not familiar with the 1942 film classic *Casablanca* starring Humphrey Bogart and Ingrid Bergman, as well as the *film noir* genre, it is strongly suggested that you watch the movie and a film noir title before proceeding. The attitudes expressed here are not necessarily those of the author.

and deadly." Arduino clasped his hands together and smiled. "Trouble? No trouble! You've come to the right place. Tell me more about this *trouble*." "Well, I've got to control a bunch of devices; LEDs, motors, actuators, the usual crew", she started, "and I've got to obtain some information from the person running the system, you know the kind, a real operator. Lots of settings; pushbuttons, switches, potentiometers, the whole megillah. I tell ya, I'm in over my head."

Arduino walked across the office and nibbled at some biscotti. He turned back to her, the twice-baked biscuit still at his fingertips, held softly the way an orchestra conductor might balance a baton. "This application…" he said, his head slightly raised and cocked to one side revealing the beginning of a knowing smile, "…it needs to be flexible, expandable and inexpensive, too?" He had piqued the dame's interest but she couldn't let it show. "Yes. Yes it does", she responded coolly. "In that case", said Arduino, "allow me to introduce Uno, the One." He tossed the remnants of the biscotti to Rick and picked up a small blue printed circuit board containing a few ICs, a bunch of headers with numbered pins and what looked like USB and power connectors.

"Pretty spiffy", she said. "What is it?" Arduino's eyes lit up. "It's an open source microcontroller development board, and when I say 'open source' I mean both software *and* hardware. The software distribution includes extensive examples, complete library source code, and all the data you could want on the AVR." "What's an AVR?" came the dame's reply. "AVR is a line of microcontrollers from Atmel. The Uno uses an ATmega 328P with 32k of on-chip programmable flash memory, 2k of SRAM data memory and 1k of EEPROM. 32 general purpose registers. Pipelined Reduced Instruction Set Computer with Harvard architecture. Most instructions require only one tick of the 16 MHz clock." Arduino's concentration was broken by a hissing sound coming from behind a large stack of books. "Ahhh! Can I interest either of you in a cup of espresso?" he asked. "Never after lunch", said Rick. He knew Arduino's hyper-caffeinated concoction would have him bouncing off the walls all afternoon. "And you, Miss Seesi?" Arduino queried. "Maybe just this once," she relied, "with milk." Arduino smiled. "Cappuccino it is!"

Sipping the steaming beverage, she looked over the board intently. "The labeled port pins on the headers are convenient- seems pretty small though. Are you sure it can handle the job?" she asked. "No problem!" said Arduino. He pulled out a couple of slightly crumpled and dog-eared pieces of paper from under a stack of CD-ROMs and placed them on the desk. First was a block diagram of the 328P as used on the Uno, the second a more detailed schematic of the board:

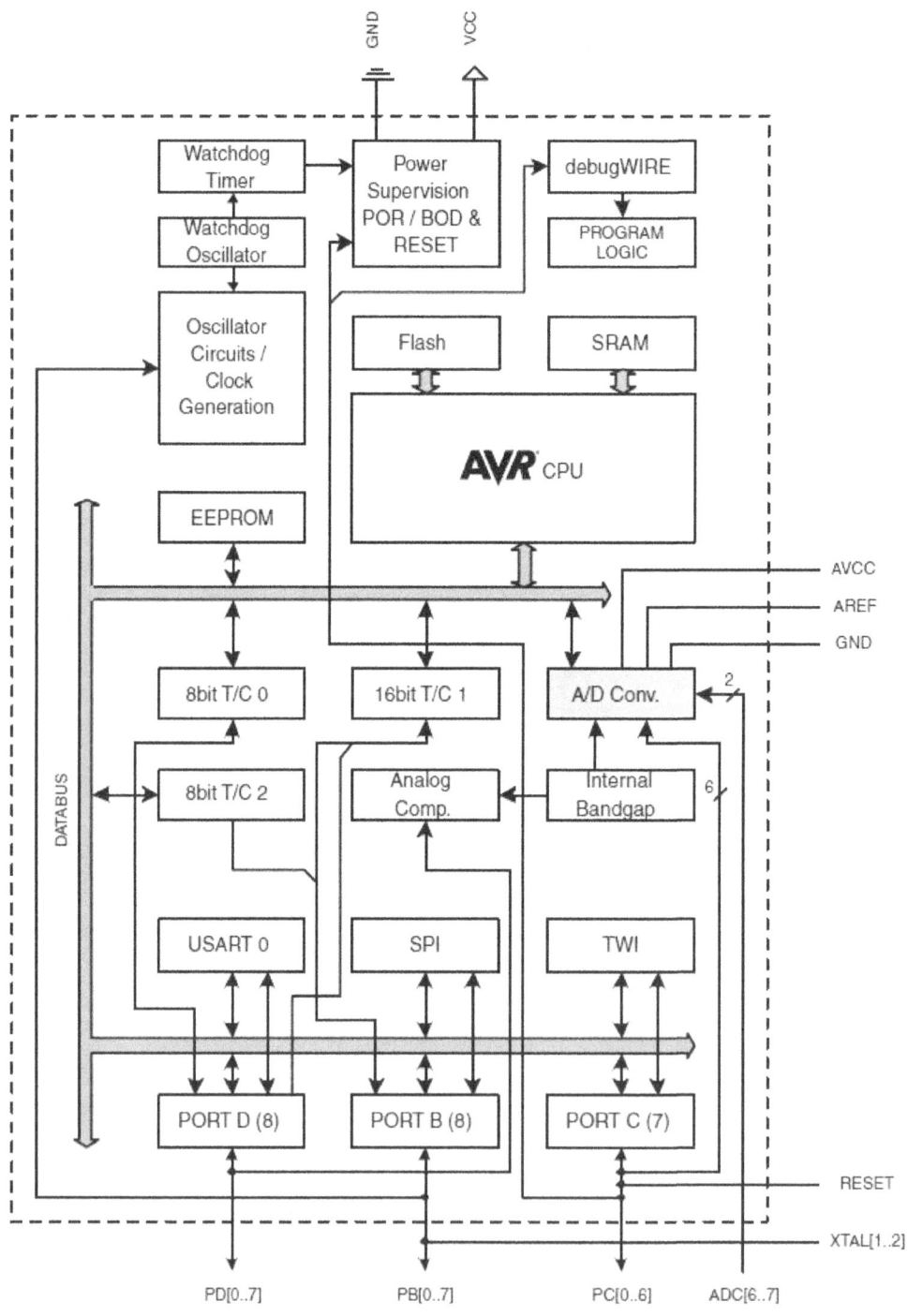

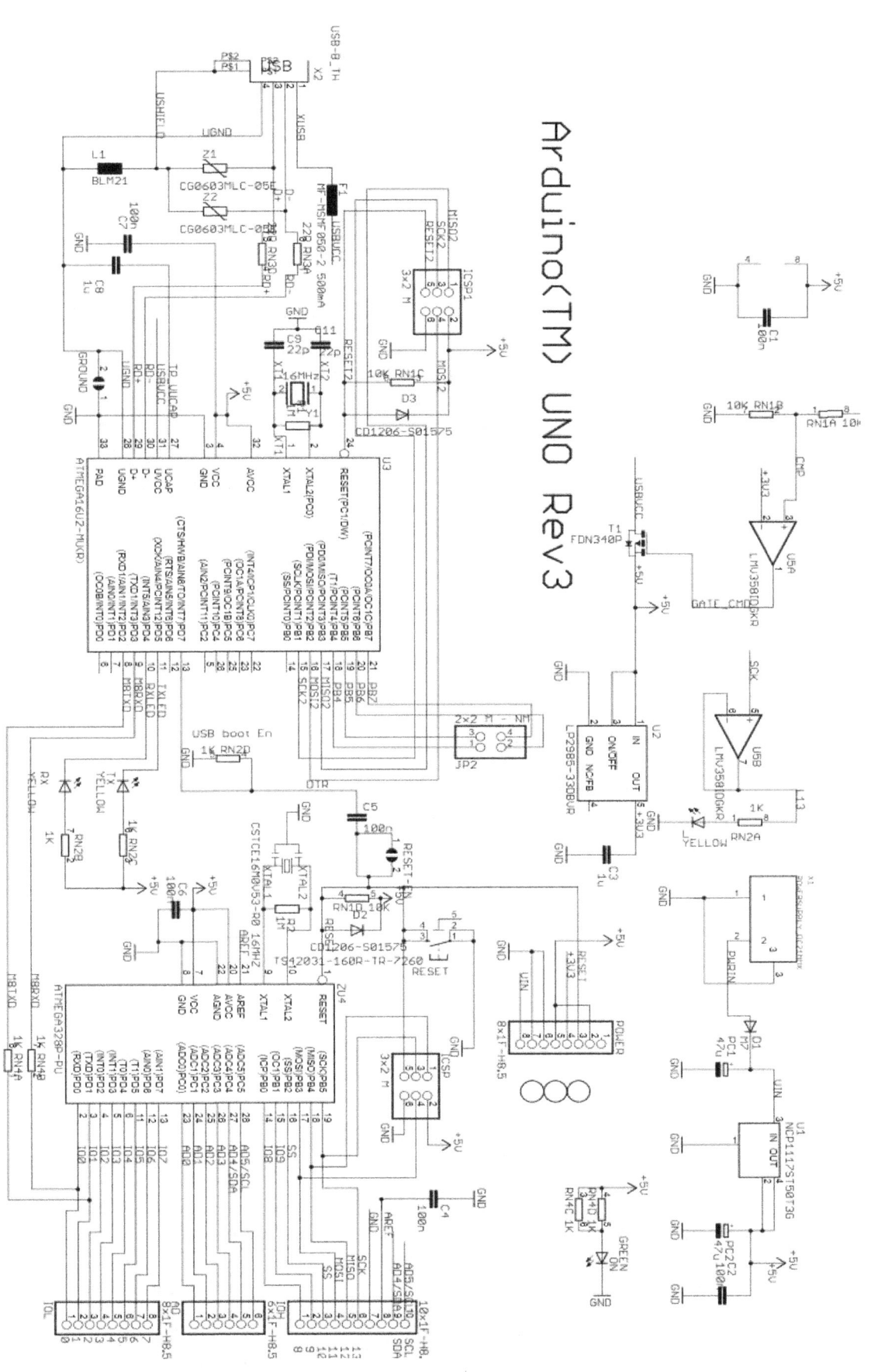

Embedded Controllers

"You've got access to three IO ports", he began, "B, C and D. Digital IO with programmable pull-down resistor. All IO is memory mapped so you can read from and write to external devices as if they were just ordinary variables using the C programming language. A Universal Synchronous-Asynchronous Receiver-Transmitter, or USART, already programmed to communicate with a host computer via USB." She interrupted him. "So I can send text back and forth between the two? That would make debugging pretty easy." "You bet!" said Arduino, obviously getting excited. "Not only that, but you've got six 10 bit analog to digital converter channels and three timer-counters; two eight bit and one 16 bit. Plus, six outputs can generate pulse width modulation signals." "What about interrupts?" she asked. "I'll need interrupts." "Multiple levels," said Arduino, "internal and external. There's a reset button already on the board."

"What about power?" she asked. "Multiple options", said Arduino. "You can power it from the USB cable. You know, USB will supply up to 100 mA to an un-enumerated device and up to 500 mA to an enumerated device. If that's not enough, you can also plug in an external supply, the wall-wart kind, or even hook in a regulated five volt source so you can supply power to relays, motors, whatever. You'd power the big wire items off-board, of course. No need to run those currents through the board traces. Whatever you choose, though, the Uno will intelligently figure out where to get its power from."

The dame was getting more interested and needed further detail. "Great, but what will the chip deliver, you know, fan out or drive." "Generally speaking," Arduino began, "the IO pins can sink or source up to 40 mA each. The entire microcontroller should be limited to 200 mA total draw to stay within thermal limits so you obviously can't drive a whole bunch of pins to maximum current capability at the same time. No big deal, that's why they make drive circuits, right?" Rick and the dame both nodded knowingly.

The office was silent as the three of them peered at the little board. The dame looked up. "What about the programming interface? Command line or IDE?" Arduino waved his hand and responded, "The IDE runs under Windows, Mac OS and Linux. You can bypass that if you want and go command line, but…" "Fine, fine", she interrupted, "and this library, it's a straight jacket, right?" "No, no!" insisted Arduino. "It's a nice library and you can use as much or as little of it as you want. Even insert assembly op codes." Assembly op codes. The thought sent a shiver down Rick's spine. He had spent a month one day trying to debug a device driver written in 8086 assembly. Never again.

It seemed that Arduino was holding something back. "Sounds good but you're not giving me the whole story are you?" she asked him. "What's the catch?" "No catch," replied Arduino, "but there's one thing. One small thing that sometimes bites the beginners." The dame raised her eyebrows and demanded, "And?"

"Like most controllers," Arduino began, "the AVR uses a memory mapped IO address for writing to a port. For example, you might write to PORTB to light an LED." "So?" the dame responded, "That's not odd." "Very true," said Arduino, "but when it comes to reading from those same physical pins, they use a different address, in this case PINB, instead of reusing PORTB."

"Wait," stammered the dame, "it's the same physical pin and if I write to it, I use PORTB but if I read from it I use PINB?"

"Don't confuse pins and ports", said Arduino as a look of melancholy crept across his face. "You must remember this, a port is just a port, a pin is just a pin. The fundamental things apply, as the clock ticks by." The dame was shaken. "But I…" she started. "Look, you gotta get the IO straight, understand?" said Arduino. His expression grew serious and he looked at her squarely. "You gotta get it plain or you'll regret it. Maybe not today, maybe not tomorrow, but soon and for the rest of your life!" Her hand brushed lightly across the Uno as she turned, and wiping a tear from her eye, she headed out the office door. Rick watched as she walked briskly down the hall. Some distance past the lab her silhouette disappeared into a fog that had mysteriously formed out of nowhere accompanied by the dull roar of a DC3's idling engines.

"She's got the Uno", said Rick. Arduino nodded, "Yes, I know. I've got plenty more where that one came from. All I need is a good lab tech to help me build more prototypes for Project Falcon using them. You interested?" A wry smile grew on Rick's face. "This Falcon, is it Maltese?" "Why yes, yes it is" came the response. "Arduino," Rick said, "I think this is the beginning of a beautiful friendship."[12]

---

[12] Complete information on the Arduino Uno development board may be found at http://arduino.cc/en/Main/ArduinoBoardUno

The Arduino system language reference may be found at http://arduino.cc/en/Reference/HomePage

Arduino tutorial info may be found at http://arduino.cc/en/Tutorial/HomePage

Arduino software downloads are found here: http://arduino.cc/en/Main/Software

When in doubt, just go here: http://www.arduino.cc and start looking.

18. Bits & Pieces: #include and #define

18.1 Introduction

Welcome to Bits & Pieces (catchy name, eh?). This sequence of chapters delves into a variety of aspects of programming the Atmel AVR ATmega 328P microcontroller via the Arduino Uno board and associated libraries. The focus is on IO (Input-Output) programming. Specifically, we'll be looking at ways of coding the interface between the Uno and external circuitry. This is code-only; the hardware aspect is dealt with separately in lab. We will be exploring the IO code used to read to and write from digital and analog ports so that we can perform tasks such as reading the state of switches, lighting LEDs, reading continuously variable data such as force or temperature, timing or counting events, and controlling devices such as motors. The simplest way of performing these items is via the library functions that come with the Arduino system[13]. Sometimes, though, these functions are not fast or efficient enough, or we need to use a non-Arduino platform. For those reasons, we'll be diving down into the library functions themselves to see how they work. To the uninitiated, scouring through library source code can be a daunting task, so think of Bits & Pieces as a series of guided tours covering major parts of the library. Granted, it's probably not as much fun as, say, a series of guided tours of tropical islands of the South Pacific, but you can only get so much for your tuition. And while there is little doubt that there might be interesting uses for embedded controllers on said islands, a field trip is *right out*.

The first things we need to examine are some commonly used include files. Recall that include files (also known as header files, i.e., the ones that end in ".h") are used to collect up function prototypes, references to global variables, structure definitions, and those wonderful (and sometimes confusing) `#define`s. Remember, the C language is fairly "skinny" and the functions that we call are either written by us or come from a library. Prototypes for the functions are found in the library's header file. An interesting twist to this is that some so-called library functions aren't functions at all. Instead, they are simply inline expansions via `#define`s. Many different libraries are available, so to make life even easier, systems often include a "master" include file that contains directives to reference other include files (boy, those professional programmers are constantly looking for ways to make every keystroke count).

18.2 Universal Stuff, Common to All Controllers

Let's start with the biggie: `arduino.h`. Here are the first few lines (some parts omitted):

```
#ifndef Arduino_h
#define Arduino_h

#include <stdlib.h>
#include <string.h>
#include <math.h>

#include <avr/pgmspace.h>
#include <avr/io.h>
#include <avr/interrupt.h>
#include "binary.h"
#define HIGH   0x1
```

---

[13] Complete details on the library and lots of other goodies including example code can be found at www.arduino.cc. The Reference page in particular will prove useful.

```
#define LOW        0x0
#define true       0x1
#define false      0x0

#define INPUT         0x0
#define OUTPUT        0x1
#define INPUT_PULLUP  0x2

#define PI         3.1415926535897932384626433832795
#define HALF_PI    1.5707963267948966192313216916398
#define TWO_PI     6.283185307179586476925286766559
#define DEG_TO_RAD 0.017453292519943295769236907684886
#define RAD_TO_DEG 57.295779513082320876798154814105
```

The first two lines prevent accidental re-entry. That is, if the file has already been included it won't be included again (if it was, you'd get a whole bunch of redefinition errors). After this we see a selection of other commonly used library header files and then a series of constant definitions. There's nothing too crazy yet. Following this are a series of what look like functions but which are inline expansions. That is, the preprocessor replaces your "function call" with a different bit of code. This is done because inline expansions do not incur the overhead of function calls and thus run faster and use less memory. Notice how some of these make use of the ternary if/else construct, such as `min()`, while others make use of recently defined constants (`radians()`). Some, such as `noInterruprs()`, perform a substitution which itself will perform a further substitution (in this case, the `cli()` "function" will turn into a single assembly language instruction that turns off interrupts globally).

```
#define min(a,b)     ((a)<(b)?(a):(b))
#define max(a,b)     ((a)>(b)?(a):(b))
#define abs(x)       ((x)>0?(x):-(x))
#define constrain(amt,low,high) ((amt)<(low)?(low):((amt)>(high)?(high):(amt)))
#define round(x)     ((x)>=0?(long)((x)+0.5):(long)((x)-0.5))
#define radians(deg) ((deg)*DEG_TO_RAD)
#define degrees(rad) ((rad)*RAD_TO_DEG)
#define sq(x)        ((x)*(x))

#define interrupts()   sei()
#define noInterrupts() cli()

#define clockCyclesPerMicrosecond() ( F_CPU / 1000000L )
```

Further down we find some `typedefs`, namely `uint8_t`, which is shorthand for an unsigned 8 bit integer, i.e., an `unsigned char`. This `typedef` was written in another header file but notice that we now have new `typedefs` based on that original `typedef` in the third and fourth lines! Thus, an `unsigned char` may now be declared merely as `boolean` or `byte`, and finally, an `unsigned int` may be declared as a `word`.

```
#define lowByte(w)  ((uint8_t) ((w) & 0xff))
#define highByte(w) ((uint8_t) ((w) >> 8))
typedef uint8_t boolean;
typedef uint8_t byte;
typedef unsigned int word;
```

Common procedures in IO programming include checking, setting and clearing specific bits in special registers. Typically this is done through bitwise math operators. For example, if you want to set the 0th bit of a register called DDRB while leaving all other bits intact, you'd bitwise OR it with 0x01 as in:

```
DDRB = DDRB | 0x01;
```

You could also define specific bit positions like so:

```
#define LEDBIT   0
#define MOTORBIT 1
#define ALARMBIT 2
```

So if you want to set the bit for the motor, you would write:

```
DDRB = DDRB | (0x01<<MOTORBIT);
```

In other words, left shift a one in the zero bit location one place (resulting in the 1st vs. 0th bit being high) and OR the register contents with it. This is a little cumbersome unless you turn it into a function call:

```
bitSet( DDRB, MOTORBIT );
```

Now that's pretty easy and obvious, so check out the lines below:

```
#define bitRead(value, bit) (((value) >> (bit)) & 0x01)
#define bitSet(value, bit) ((value) |= (1UL << (bit)))
#define bitClear(value, bit) ((value) &= ~(1UL << (bit)))
#define bitWrite(value, bit, bitvalue) (bitvalue ? bitSet(value, bit) : bitClear(value, bit))

#define bit(b) (1UL << (b))
```

Further along in the file we come across a bunch of function prototypes for items we will be using:

```
void pinMode(uint8_t, uint8_t);
void digitalWrite(uint8_t, uint8_t);
int  digitalRead(uint8_t);
int  analogRead(uint8_t);
void analogReference(uint8_t mode);
void analogWrite(uint8_t, int);

unsigned long millis(void);
unsigned long micros(void);
void delay(unsigned long);
void setup(void);
void loop(void);
```

The last two are particularly important. The Arduino development system has a pre-written `main()` function. It makes calls to `setup()` and `loop()`, so we'll be writing these as our primary entry points.

18.3 Controller Specific Stuff

Moving on to other header files, we must recall that there are dozens and dozens of models in a given processor series like the AVR. Each of these controllers will have different memory capacities, IO capabilities and so forth, so we need to distinguish which one we're using while also trying to keep the code as generic as possible. Normally, this is done by creating specific header files for each controller. The IDE then gives you an option to select which controller you're using and #defines a controller ID for it (see the list in the Arduino IDE under *Tools>>Board*). Consider the following chunk of avr/io.h:

```
#ifndef _AVR_IO_H_
#define _AVR_IO_H_

#include <avr/sfr_defs.h>
```

We find a (huge) series of conditional includes, each looking for the one pre-defined processor symbol set by the Arduino IDE:

```
#if defined (__AVR_AT94K__)
#  include <avr/ioat94k.h>
#elif defined (__AVR_AT43USB320__)
#  include <avr/io43u32x.h>
#elif defined (__AVR_AT43USB355__)
#  include <avr/io43u35x.h>
```

… and so on until we get to the ATmega 328P for the Arduino Uno:

```
#elif defined (__AVR_ATmega328P__)
#  include <avr/iom328p.h>
```

… and we continue until we get to the end:

```
#elif defined (__AVR_ATxmega256A3B__)
#  include <avr/iox256a3b.h>
#else
#  if !defined(__COMPILING_AVR_LIBC__)
#    warning "device type not defined"
#  endif
#endif

#include <avr/portpins.h>
#include <avr/common.h>
#include <avr/version.h>

#endif /* _AVR_IO_H_ */
```

So what's in avr/iom328p.h you ask? This includes a bunch of things that will make our programming lives much easier such as definitions for ports, registers and bits. We're going to be seeing these over and over:

```
#ifndef _AVR_IOM328P_H_
#define _AVR_IOM328P_H_ 1
```

Embedded Controllers

```
/* Registers and associated bit numbers */
```

This is an 8 bit input port and associated bits

```
#define PINB   _SFR_IO8(0x03)
#define PINB0  0
#define PINB1  1
#define PINB2  2
#define PINB3  3
#define PINB4  4
#define PINB5  5
#define PINB6  6
#define PINB7  7
```

This is an 8 bit data direction register and associated bits

```
#define DDRB   _SFR_IO8(0x04)
#define DDB0   0
#define DDB1   1
#define DDB2   2
#define DDB3   3
#define DDB4   4
#define DDB5   5
#define DDB6   6
#define DDB7   7
```

This is an 8 bit output port and associated bits

```
#define PORTB   _SFR_IO8(0x05)
#define PORTB0  0
#define PORTB1  1
#define PORTB2  2
#define PORTB3  3
#define PORTB4  4
#define PORTB5  5
#define PORTB6  6
#define PORTB7  7
```

…and so on for ports C and D. Now for analog to digital converter (ADC) goodies:

```
#ifndef __ASSEMBLER__
#define ADC     _SFR_MEM16(0x78)
#endif
#define ADCW    _SFR_MEM16(0x78)

#define ADCL   _SFR_MEM8(0x78)
#define ADCL0  0
#define ADCL1  1
#define ADCL2  2
#define ADCL3  3
#define ADCL4  4
#define ADCL5  5
#define ADCL6  6
#define ADCL7  7
```

```
#define ADCH   _SFR_MEM8(0x79)
#define ADCH0  0
#define ADCH1  1
#define ADCH2  2
#define ADCH3  3
#define ADCH4  4
#define ADCH5  5
#define ADCH6  6
#define ADCH7  7

#define ADCSRA _SFR_MEM8(0x7A)
#define ADPS0  0
#define ADPS1  1
#define ADPS2  2
#define ADIE   3
#define ADIF   4
#define ADATE  5
#define ADSC   6
#define ADEN   7

#define ADCSRB _SFR_MEM8(0x7B)
#define ADTS0  0
#define ADTS1  1
#define ADTS2  2
#define ACME   6

#define ADMUX  _SFR_MEM8(0x7C)
#define MUX0   0
#define MUX1   1
#define MUX2   2
#define MUX3   3
#define ADLAR  5
#define REFS0  6
#define REFS1  7
```

… and so on for the remainder of the header file. OK, so just what is this nugget below?

```
#define PORTB  _SFR_IO8(0x05)
```

Most controllers communicate via *memory-mapped IO*. That is, external pins are written to and read from as if they are ordinary memory locations. So if you want to write to a port, you can simply declare a pointer variable, set its value to the appropriate address, and then manipulate it as needed. For the ATmega 328P, the address of IO Port B is 0x25. You could write the following if you wanted to set bit 5 high:

```
unsigned char *portB;

portB = (unsigned char *)0x25; // cast required to keep compiler quiet
*portB = *portB | 0x20;
```

You could also use the bit setting function seen earlier which is a little clearer:

```
bitSet( *portB, 5 );
```

Embedded Controllers

The problem here is that you have to declare and use the pointer variable which is a little clunky. There's also the error-prone business of pointer de-referencing in the assignment statement (the * in front of the variable which beginning programmers tend to forget). Besides, it requires that you look up the specific address of the port (and change it if you use another processor). So to make things more generic we place the addresses (or more typically, offsets from a base address) in the processor-specific header file.

The header file declares an item, PORTB, for our convenience. It is defined as _SFR_IO8(0x05) but what's that _SFR_IO8 function? In sfr_defs.h it's defined as follows:

```
#define _SFR_IO8(io_addr) _MMIO_BYTE((io_addr) + __SFR_OFFSET)
```

and __SFR_OFFSET is defined as 0x20. In other words, this item is 0x05 above the base offset address of 0x20, meaning it's the address 0x25 as we saw earlier. But what the heck is _MMIO_BYTE()? That looks a little weird at first glance:

```
#define _MMIO_BYTE(mem_addr) (*(volatile uint8_t *)(mem_addr))
```

This is just a cast with a pointer de-reference. It says this item is a pointer to an unsigned char which is being de-referenced (de-referenced by the first * and don't forget the earlier typedef for the uint8_t). By placing all of these items in header files we've managed to make the IO programming generic while at the same time removing the need for pointer variable declarations and the need for pointer de-referencing[14].

Therefore, if we want to set bit 5 high, we can now just say

```
PORTB = PORTB | 0x20;   // or more typically: PORTB |= 0x20;
```

or

```
bitSet( PORTB, 5 );    // note lack of "*" in both lines of code
```

All the business about exactly where PORTB is located in the memory map is hidden from us and there will be no accidental errors due to leaving out the *. The same code will work with several different processors, and to top it off, it's operationally more efficient than dealing with pointers as well. Consequently, we will normally use these symbolic register and port names rather than hard addresses in future work. Simply lovely. Time for a snack; something fruity perhaps, something that reminds us of tropical islands…

---

[14] If you're wondering about volatile, recall that it's a modifier that indicates that the variable can be changed by another process (possibly an interrupt). This will prevent overly aggressive assembly code optimizations by the compiler.

19. Bits & Pieces: Digital Output Circuitry

19.1 Introduction

To fully appreciate the software interface to microcontrollers and to gain insight into how to interface controllers to external devices, it is useful to examine the underlying circuitry. In this chapter we shall investigate the basic digital output circuitry. Anything that can be controlled with a simple logical yes/no, true/false input can be a target. Although controllers usually have limited output current and voltage capability, they can control devices such as power transistors which can in turn control more demanding loads. A simplified diagram of the General Purpose Input-Output (GPIO) circuitry can be seen in Figure 19.1.

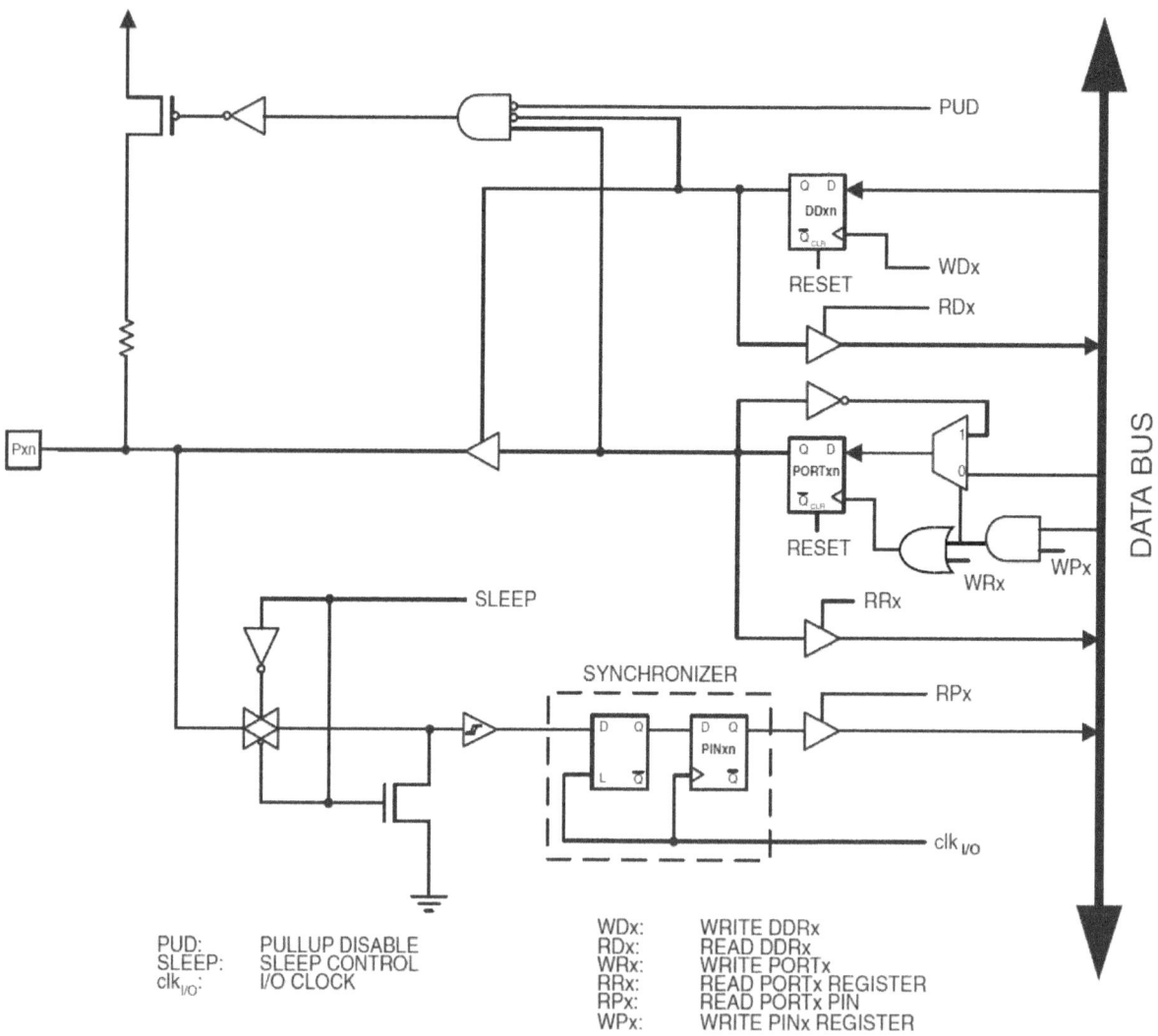

Figure 19.1, GPIO circuitry (from Atmel 2014)

The circuit represents a single bit. An IO port consists of eight bits, typically. Therefore this circuitry would be replicated seven more times to accommodate a single byte-wide port, of which there may be several. Also, in order to reduce the external pin count of the IC, pins may be multiplexed with other functions. The multiplexers are not shown in this schematic. Pxn, at the far left of the schematic, represents the physical output pin. The data bus shown along the right edge is the source for data being written to the physical pin and also the destination for data being read from the pin. For now we shall focus on writing to the output and examine input functionality in a later chapter. While this circuit is specific to the ATmega series, it is representative of GPIO circuitry found in many microcontrollers.

19.2 Output Circuitry

Figure 19.2 presents a further simplification focusing solely on the output portion.

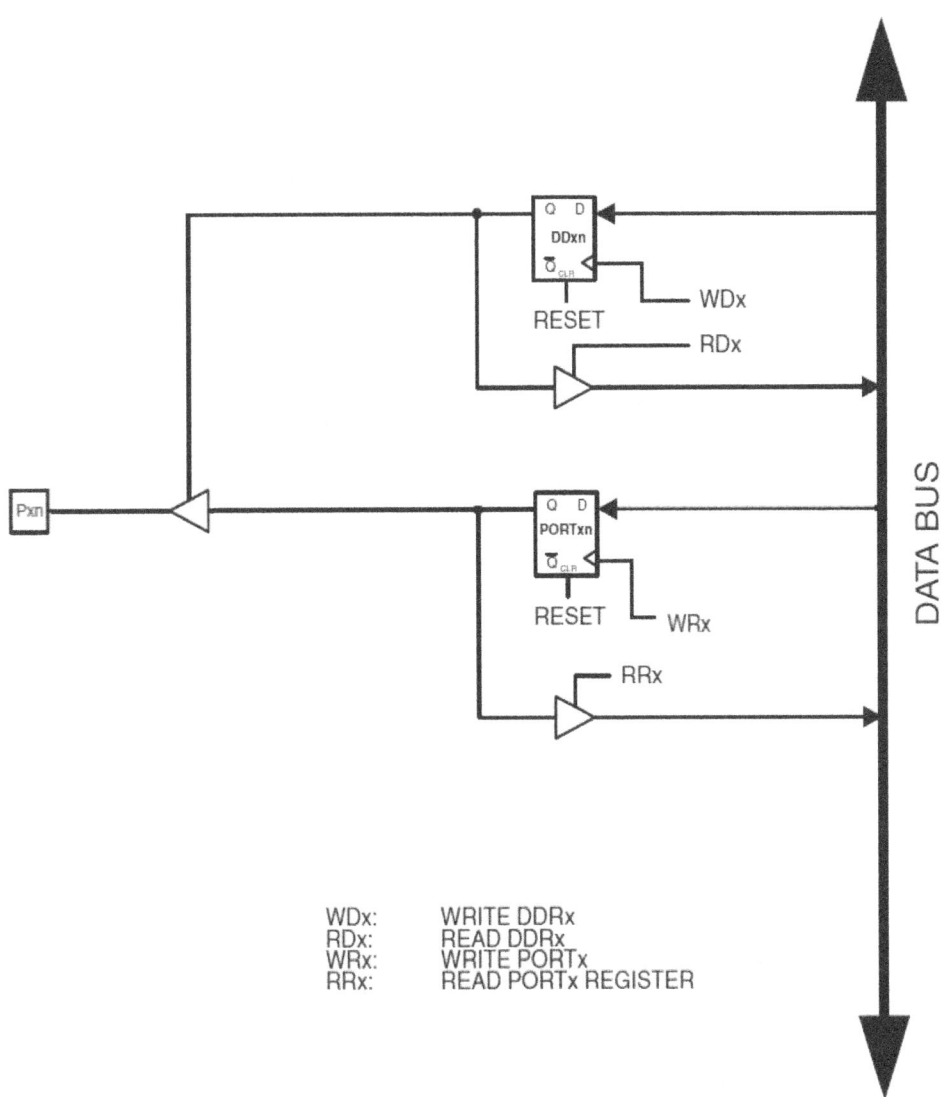

Figure 19.2, output circuitry simplified (from Atmel 2014)

Embedded Controllers

First off, the PUD (Pull Up Disable), SLEEP and CLK (CLocK) control lines are common to all bits and ports. We may ignore them for our purposes. The lowest section is removed because it is involved with input functionality. The same goes for the upper section surrounding the MOSFET. Finally, a series of two gates, an inverter and a multiplexer clustered around the middle section have been removed. These serve a particular (and perhaps somewhat esoteric) function, namely the ability to rapidly toggle a bit. Again, this section is not needed for typical functioning.

Upon simplification we are left with a circuit that centers around two D flip-flops and a few tri-state buffers. The primary signals of interest are WDx and WRx which feed the DDxn and PORTxn flip-flops. DDxn is the Data Direction bit. It determines whether the physical pin is configured for output (writing) or input (reading). PORTxn presents the data that needs to be written. Note that the "x" refers to the port letter, as in Port B, while the "n" refers to the bit number within that port. Thus, the physical pin for bit number two in Port B would be denoted here as PB2 (or alternately, PORTB.2). The collection of all eight bits of DDxn is referred to as the Data Direction Register, or DDR. The Data Direction Register for Port B would be referred to as DDRB. Each port will have these registers mapped in memory. That is, for Port B there will be a DDRB for direction control and a PORTB for writing data (there is also a PINB for reading, more on that later). Similarly there will a DDRC and PORTC (and PINC) for Port C, and so on for as many ports as the controller has (B, C and D for the ATmega 328P).

To understand how the circuit works, recall that a D flip-flop's Q output simply echoes the logic level present at the D input when the control signal transitions from low to high (i.e., positive edge trigger). Note that the output of PORTxn feeds a tri-state buffer which in turn feeds the physical pin. In order to write data to the pin, a logic high is first placed on the data bus. The WDx signal is pulsed which transfers the logic high to Q of DDxn. This high level enables the tri-state buffer connected to Pxn. The port bit is now configured for output and it will stay in this mode until WDx is re-asserted. The desired data (high or low bit) is now placed on the data bus. The WRx signal is pulsed which transfers the logic level to Q of PORTxn. This feeds the afore-mentioned tri-state which transfers the data bit to the output. This level will remain until WRx is re-asserted. If WDx and WRx are never re-asserted, the output pin level will never change. In order to write new data to the output pin, the desired data bit is placed on the bus and WRx is pulsed. It is not necessary to re-load DDxn and re-assert WDx each time.

For example, suppose we wish to flash an LED several times. We could do this by attaching an LED to the pin and then toggling the pin from high to low repeatedly. First, we would write a high to DDxn to establish output (write) mode. Then we would write a high to PORTxn, turning on the LED. After a short wait we would write a low to PORTxn, turning off the LED. After a further short wait we would write another high to PORTxn (turning the LED back on) and continue the process in like manner for as many flashes as we need.

The final two tri-state buffers associated with the RDx and RRx signals allow us to read the current states of the direction and port bits.

20. Bits & Pieces: Digital Input Circuitry

20.1 Introduction

In this chapter we shall investigate the basic digital input circuitry. This can be used to sense the state of external switches and other two-state devices. These devices can be active, that is, generating a high or low voltage, or they can be simple passive switches connecting to ground through the use of an optional internal pull-up resistor. A simplified diagram of the General Purpose Input-Output (GPIO) circuitry can be seen in Figure 20.1. As in the previous chapter, this is for a single bit. Once again, we shall remove sections that are not pertinent to the input function or for enhanced clarity.

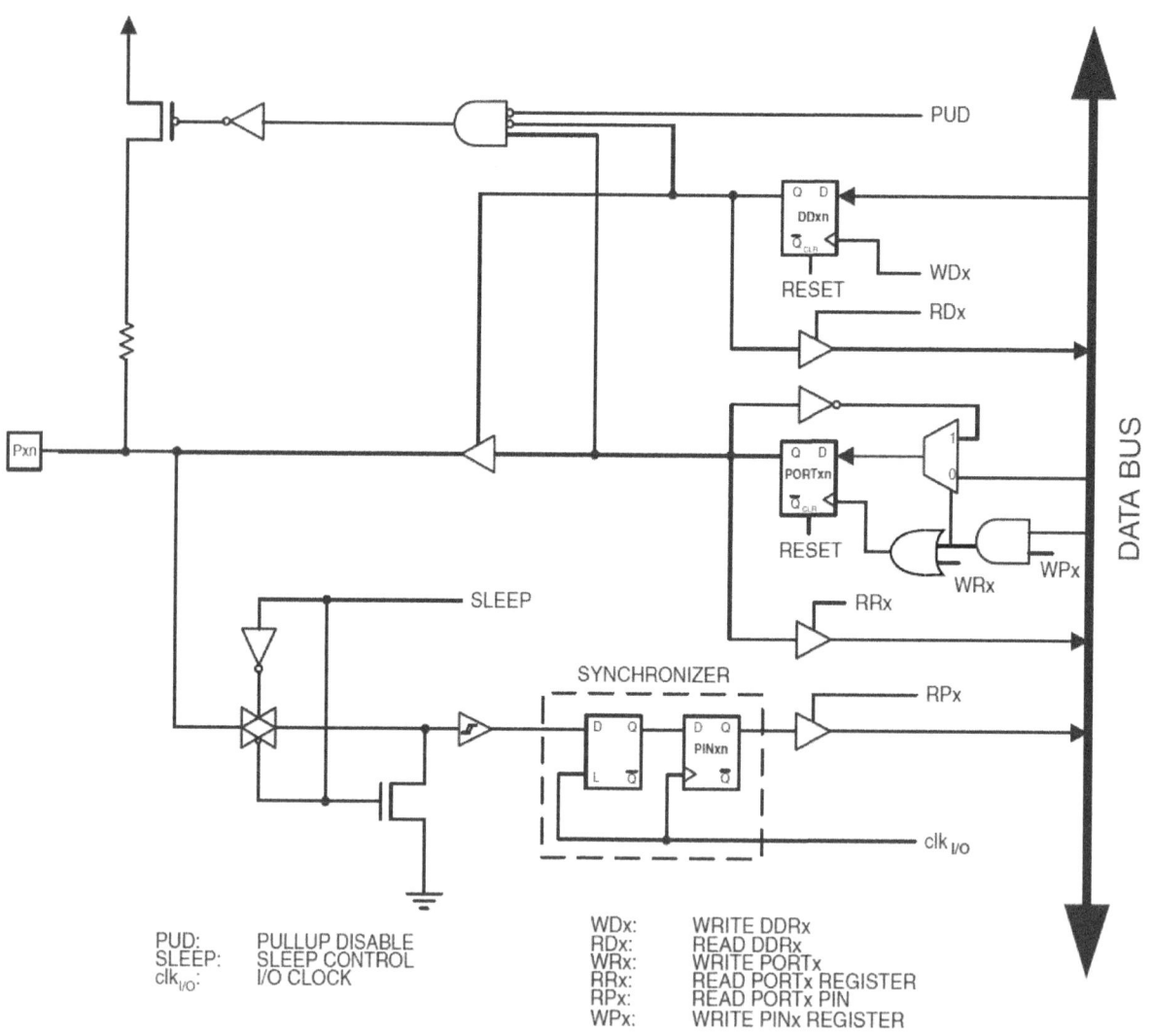

Figure 20.1, GPIO circuitry (from Atmel 2014)

20.2 Input Circuitry

Figure 20.2 presents a further simplification focusing solely on the input portion.

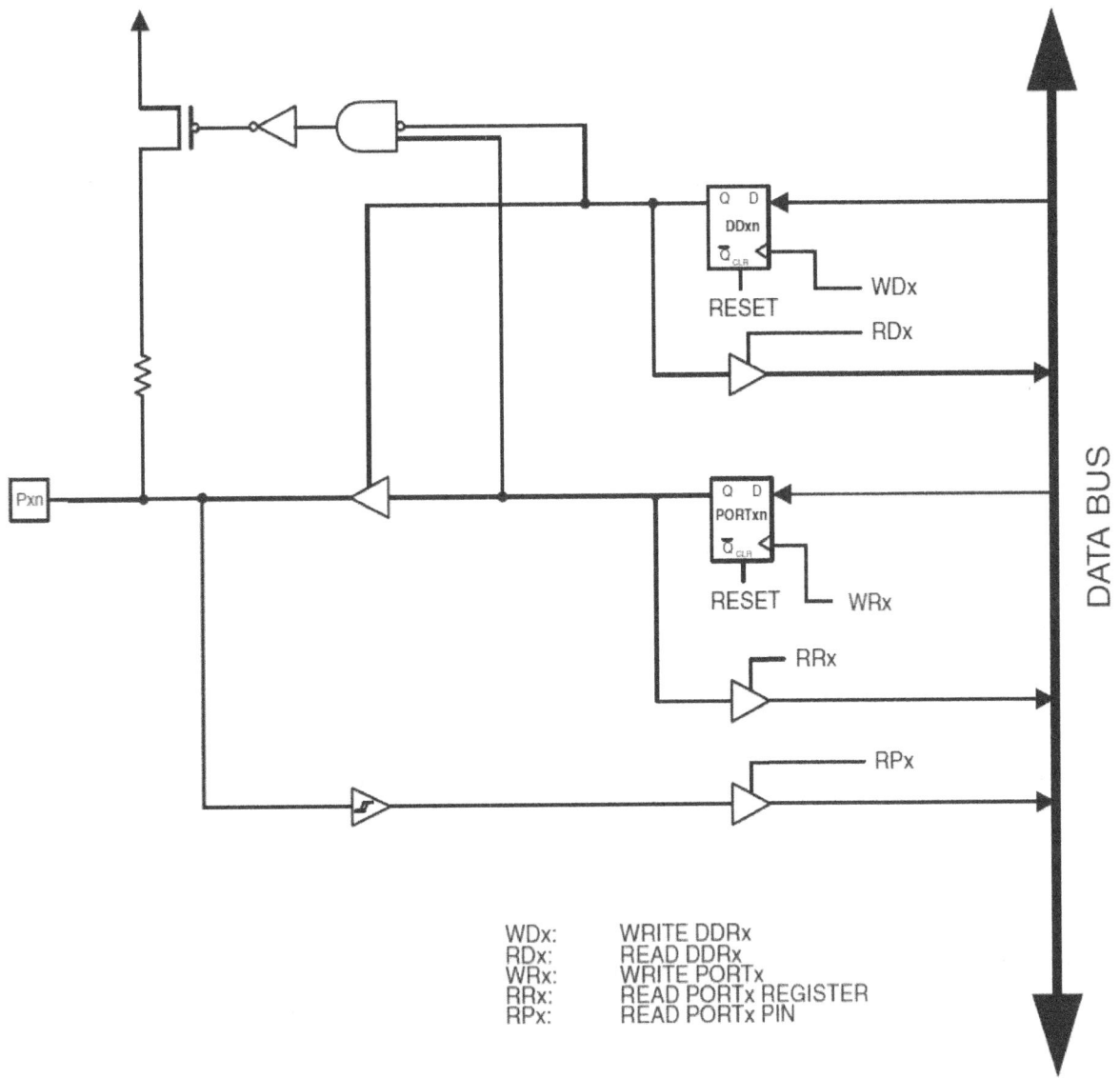

Figure 20.2, input circuitry simplified (from Atmel 2014)

Once again we have removed the gates surrounding PORTxn that create the bit toggle function. Further, we have removed the PUD, SLEEP and CLK signals and simplified the lower section leaving just the Schmitt Trigger. The read process will be similar to the write process examined in the previous chapter.

To read a signal on an external pin, we will need to write a logic low to the data direction bit DDxn. This will disconnect PORTxn from the physical pin, Pxn, because the tri-state buffer will go to high-Z state. If

Embedded Controllers

PORTxn was left connected, the external device would wind up trying to drive the active output of PORTxn. This would produce unpredictable results at best.

Now that PORTxn is disconnected from Pxn, the signal existing at Pxn drives the Schmitt Trigger located along the bottom edge of the diagram. This signal will be passed on to the data bus once the RPx (Read Pin x) control signal is asserted on the lower tri-state buffer. A Schmitt Trigger is used as an intermediary here as we cannot be certain of clean, noise-free input signals. Also, note that the input signals are read from a PIN register (e.g., PINB or PINC). This is in contrast to the PORT registers used when writing data. Thus, if you want to write data to the outside world, you write to a PORT register. If you want to read data from the outside world, you read from a PIN register. Not all microcontrollers use this naming convention. Some use a single PORT register for both writing and reading. A good mnemonic for remembering whether PIN or PORT is used for input or output is to associate the "in" in PIN and the "o" (for output) in PORT. Typically, the PORT, PIN and DDR registers are adjacent in the memory map. For example, using port B we find PINB at 0x23, DDRB at 0x24 and PORTB at 0x25. Check the register map in the Appendix for more.

We are still left with the MOSFET section. This is used to generate an optional pull-up resistor. There are two basic ways to generate input signals. The first is with an active circuit. For example, the output of a logic gate could be connected to the external pin. The voltage produced by the gate would be fed to the Schmitt Trigger as described previously and the signal would make its way to the data bus. It is not always convenient to generate an external voltage with an active circuit, though. If you wanted to read the state of a simple push button, you couldn't just connect it between the pin and ground as there would be no signal to sense. Instead you'd have to connect it to an external power supply through a limiting resistor, requiring more components and space. The pull-up takes care of this for you. When activated, the MOSFET connects its associated resistor to the internal power line. If a switch is now connected between the external pin and ground, and is closed, the pin is pulled to ground (i.e., logic low). If the switch is opened, the resistor "pulls up" the pin voltage to the supply rail (i.e., logic high). Thus, we can determine the state of the switch with no other external circuitry.

To activate the pull-up, first the pin must be in input mode (DDxn at logic low which feeds the AND gate). Also, the output of PORTxn must be logic high. These two signals will drive the AND gate's output high, turning on the MOSFET and engaging the pull-up resistor. It might seem a little odd to be writing to the PORT bit for read mode but this is just a neat way of making the most of the available hardware. After all, in read mode, the PORT register is otherwise unused. Why let it go to waste and require yet another register to control the pull-up?

In summary, to read from the external pin, a low is written to the appropriate DDR bit, placing this circuit in read (input) mode. If a pull-up is desired, a high is written to the appropriate PORT bit. If a pull-up is not desired, a low is written to the PORT bit. Once this is done, the external value can be read from the PIN register. As with the output circuitry, the DDR and PORT do not have to be rewritten prior to each subsequent read from the PIN. The D flip-flops will hold their values until they are rewritten, thus maintaining the current data direction and pull-up status.

21. Bits & Pieces: pinMode()

Or "Programming Port Directions and Your Bicycle"

In this tour, we're going to start looking at digital IO. Digital IO will allow us to read the state of an input pin as well as produce a logical high or low at an output pin. Examples include reading the state of an external switch and turning an LED or motor on and off.

If every potential external connection between a microcontroller and the outside world had a dedicated wire, the pin count for controller packages would be huge. The ATmega 328P in the Uno board has four 8 bit ports plus connections for power, ground and the like, yet it only has 28 physical pins. How is this possible? Simple, we'll *multiplex* the pins, that is, make multiple uses for each. If, for example, we were to look at the 0th bit of IO port B, this leads to a single external pin. This pin can be programmed to behave in either input (read) mode or output (write) mode. In general, each bit of a port can be programmed independently; some for input, some for output, or all of them the same. Obviously, before we use a port we need to tell the controller which way it should behave. In the Arduino system this is usually done via a call to the library function `pinMode()`. Here is the description of the function from the on-line reference[15]:

---

pinMode()

Description

Configures the specified pin to behave either as an input or an output. See the description of digital pins for details on the functionality of the pins.

As of Arduino 1.0.1, it is possible to enable the internal pullup resistors with the mode INPUT_PULLUP. Additionally, the INPUT mode explicitly disables the internal pullups.

Syntax

pinMode(pin, mode)

Parameters

pin: the number of the pin whose mode you wish to set

mode: INPUT, OUTPUT, or INPUT_PULLUP. (see the digital pins page for a more complete description of the functionality.)

Returns

None

Figure 21.1, pinMode docs

[15] http://www.arduino.cc/en/Reference/PinMode

So we'd first have to think in terms of an Arduino pin number instead of a port bit number. Below is a table of Arduino Uno pin designations versus ATmega 328P port and pin naming.

Arduino Designator	General Purpose IO Designator	Comment
A0	PORTC bit 0	ADC input 0
A1	PORTC bit 1	ADC input 1
A2	PORTC bit 2	ADC input 2
A3	PORTC bit 3	ADC input 3
A4	PORTC bit 4	ADC input 4
A5	PORTC bit 5	ADC input 5
0	PORTD bit 0	RX
1	PORTD bit 1	TX
2	PORTD bit 2	
3	PORTD bit 3	PWM
4	PORTD bit 4	
5	PORTD bit 5	PWM
6	PORTD bit 6	PWM
7	PORTD bit 7	
8	PORTB bit 0	
9	PORTB bit 1	PWM
10	PORTB bit 2	PWM
11	PORTB bit 3	PWM
12	PORTB bit 4	
13	PORTB bit 5	Built-in LED

Figure 21.2, Arduino Uno Pin Definitions

The naming convention is reasonably logical but less than perfect. Note that the A0 through A5 designators are for the analog inputs and the remaining are for digital IO. A0 through A5 are, in fact, predefined global constants that map back to numeric values (e.g., A0 is 14 for the Uno, see the file pins_arduino.h for details). It should also be noted that the analog channels are input-only. The controller cannot produce continuously variable analog voltages on its own. This is not to say that it's impossible to get analog control; just that it's going to take a little more work (as we shall see soon enough).

Practically speaking the pin naming convention isn't all that bad as the pins are labeled right on the board, see Figure 21.3.

Figure 21.3, Arduino Uno

For example, directly above the Arduino Uno logo you can spot an "8" next to a pin located at the edge of a 10 pin header. According to the table above, this is bit 0 of port B. To set this connector to output mode to drive an external circuit, you could write:

```
pinMode( 8, OUTPUT );
```

OK, so what if we're using this controller on a non-Arduino system, and is there a faster way to accomplish this (code execution-wise)? Let's take a look at the code for this function. It's found in a file called wiring_digital.c. Here are the relevant bits and pieces (slightly altered to make some portions a little more clear):

```
void pinMode(uint8_t pin, uint8_t mode)
{
    uint8_t bit, port, oldSREG;
    volatile uint8_t *reg, *out;

    bit = digitalPinToBitMask( pin );
    port = digitalPinToPort( pin );

    if (port == NOT_A_PIN) return;  // bad pin # requested

    reg = portModeRegister( port );
    out = portOutputRegister( port );
```

Embedded Controllers

```
            if (mode == INPUT)
            {
                    oldSREG = SREG;
                    cli();
                    *reg &= ~bit;
                    *out &= ~bit;
                    SREG = oldSREG;
            }
            else
            {
                    if (mode == INPUT_PULLUP)
                    {
                            oldSREG = SREG;
                            cli();
                            *reg &= ~bit;
                            *out |= bit;
                            SREG = oldSREG;
                    }
                    else // must be OUTPUT mode
                    {
                            oldSREG = SREG;
                            cli();
                            *reg |= bit;
                            SREG = oldSREG;
                    }
            }
}
```

Figure 21.4, pinMode code

After the declaration of a few local variables, the specified Arduino pin number is decoded into both a port and its associated bit mask by the `digitalPinTo...()` functions. If a pin is specified that does not exist on this particular processor, `port` will be set to an error value so we check for this and bail out if it's so. What's a port bit mask? That's just an 8 bit value with all 0s except for a 1 in the desired bit position (sometimes it's the complement of this, that is, all 1s with a 0- it depends on whether you intend to set, clear, AND or OR). The `port...Register()` functions perform similar decoding operations. For example, the so-called "port mode register" is better known as the data direction register, or DDR. The ATmega 328P has three of these, `DDRB` through `DDRD`. Setting a bit sets the mode to output (write) while clearing puts it in input (read) mode.

These four "functions" are really look-up tables disguised as functions. It's merely an access to an array filled with appropriate values. Accessing an array is much faster than calling a function. Consider the `portModeRegister()` function, which given a port designator, will return the actual data direction port which we can manipulate (e.g., DDRC). This is defined as:

```
#define portModeRegister(P)
        ( (volatile uint8_t *)( pgm_read_word( port_to_mode_PGM + (P))) )
```

`port_to_mode_PGM` turns out to be an array[16] filled with the pre-defined error symbol and the addresses of the appropriate data direction registers:

```
const uint16_t PROGMEM port_to_mode_PGM[] = {
        NOT_A_PORT,
        NOT_A_PORT,
        (uint16_t) &DDRB,
        (uint16_t) &DDRC,
        (uint16_t) &DDRD,
};
```

`pgm_read_word` is a special function used to read values from the program space versus the normal data space (remember, this controller uses a Harvard architecture with split memory).

The end result is that we'll get back the address of the required data direction register and that's what we'll need to access in order to set input or output mode.

The next chunk of code is just three if/else possibilities, one for each of the modes we could request. Let's take a look at `OUTPUT` mode first.

```
else
{
        oldSREG = SREG;
        cli();
        *reg |= bit;
        SREG = oldSREG;
}
```

Probably the single most important register on a microcontroller is the *status register*, here called `SREG`. It contains a bunch of flag bits that signify a series of states. For example, there is a bit to indicate that an arithmetic operation overflowed (i.e., there were too few bits to hold the result). There's a bit to indicate the result is negative, and so forth. One of the bits controls whether or not the system will respond to *interrupts*. An interrupt is a high priority event that can halt (interrupt) the execution of your code while the interrupt code (ISR, or interrupt service routine) runs instead. An interrupt can occur at any time, even when your code is in the middle of something important. To prevent this from happening, we first save the current contents of the status register and then clear the status bit that enables interrupts from occurring. That's the `cli()` call (which, as it turns out, is an in-line expansion to a single assembly instruction called, you guessed it, `CLI`). Once we know we won't be interrupted, we can fiddle with the DDR. `reg` is the DDR for this particular port. We OR it with the bit mask of interest, in other words, we set that bit. This selects the direction as output. Finally, we restore the original contents of the status register, enabling interrupts (assuming it had been set to begin with).

So, when originally we wrote

```
pinMode( 8, OUTPUT );
```

The function decoded Arduino pin 8 as being bit 0 of port B (i.e., `PORTB`). It also determined that the corresponding DDR is `DDRB`. The bit 0 mask is 0x01 and it was ORed with the contents of `DDRB`, thus selecting the direction for that bit as output mode.

---

[16] These are found in avr/pgmspace.h and pins_arduino.h

The clause for INPUT mode is similar:

```
if (mode == INPUT)
{
    oldSREG = SREG;
    cli();
    *reg &= ~bit;
    *out &= ~bit;
    SREG = oldSREG;
}
```

Note that here the DDR is ANDed with the complement of the bit mask to clear the bit, thus placing it in input mode. This code also clears the same bit in the output register which disables the pull-up resistor at the external pin. In contrast, note that INPUT_PULLUP mode sets this bit.

Great stuff for sure, but what if you're not using an Arduino or you need to get this done quicker? If you don't have any interrupt code running you can safely twiddle directly with the port and DDR. Remember, we wanted to make bit 0 of port B ready for output. That means we need to set bit 0 of DDRB.

```
DDRB |= 0x01;
```

or use the macro

```
bitSet( DDRB, 0 );
```

Either would do the trick, the latter probably a little more clear and less error prone. And here's something very useful to remember: What if you need to set a bunch of pins or even an entire port to input or output mode? Using pinMode() you'd have to make individual calls for each pin. In contrast, if you needed to set the bottom six bits of port B to output mode[17] you could just do this:

```
DDRB |= 0x3f;    // set Uno pins 8 through 13 to OUTPUT mode
```

Does this mean that we should never use pinMode()? No! We have seen that this function ties in perfectly with the Arduino Uno board and is both more robust and more flexible. It's just that sometimes a bicycle will serve us better than a motor vehicle and it's good that we have the option.

---

[17] You might do this in order to write values out of the port in parallel fashion, several bits at a time, for example to feed a parallel input DAC.

22. Bits & Pieces: digitalWrite()

"Writing to a port" implies that we wish to control some external device. This might involve setting or clearing a single bit to turn on an LED or motor. A set of bits might also be required, for example, to send out ASCII code byte-by-byte or to write data words to an external digital to analog converter (DAC). It is important to remember that the microcontroller has a limited amount of sink/source current available per pin (40 mA for each pin of the ATmega 328P but no more than 200 mA total for the chip). Thus, it is possible to drive a handful of LEDs to 10 mA each with a direct connection consisting of a current limiting resistor and the LED, but not possible to turn on even a relatively small DC motor. Higher current (or voltage) loads will require some manner of driver or interface circuit. We will forgo that discussion and just focus on the code portion here.

As the output port pins can only be in either a high or low state, they are referred to as digital outputs. While it is possible to generate analog signals, either through pulse width modulation or additional external circuitry, the digital high/low nature of port pins is all there is. Generally speaking, most microcontrollers do not produce continuously variable analog voltages at their port pins. There are exceptions to this, though. For example, the Arduino Due[18] board utilizes the Atmel SAM3X8E ARM Cortex-M3 CPU which contains two internal 12 bit DACs.

Before writing, the port has to be set up for the proper direction. This means using either `pinMode()` or the associated data direction register, `DDRx`, to set the mode to output **before** we can consider writing data to an external device. If a single port bit is all that's required, `pinMode()` is very straightforward and robust. If several bits need to be controlled together, it may be easier to go directly to `DDRx`.

Just as there are two methods to set the output mode, the same is true for writing the data itself; one effective method for single bits and another for sets of bits.

To write a single bit, the `digitalWrite()` function is a good choice. Here is the on-line documentation for it, found at http://arduino.cc/en/Reference/DigitalWrite:

---

digitalWrite()

Description

Write a HIGH or a LOW value to a digital pin.

If the pin has been configured as an OUTPUT with **pinMode**(), its voltage will be set to the corresponding value: 5V (or 3.3V on 3.3V boards) for HIGH, 0V (ground) for LOW.

If the pin is configured as an INPUT, writing a HIGH value with digitalWrite() will enable an internal 20K pullup resistor (see the tutorial on digital pins). Writing LOW will disable the pullup. The pullup resistor is enough to light an LED dimly, so if LEDs appear to work, but very dimly, this is a likely cause. The remedy is to set the pin to an output with the pinMode() function.

---

[18] http://arduino.cc/en/Main/ArduinoBoardDue

> **NOTE:** Digital pin 13 is harder to use as a digital input than the other digital pins because it has an LED and resistor attached to it that's soldered to the board on most boards. If you enable its internal 20k pull-up resistor, it will hang at around 1.7 V instead of the expected 5V because the onboard LED and series resistor pull the voltage level down, meaning it always returns LOW. If you must use pin 13 as a digital input, use an external pull down resistor.
>
> Syntax
>
> digitalWrite(pin, value)
>
> Parameters
>
> pin: the pin number
>
> value: HIGH or LOW
>
> Returns
>
> none
>
> Example
>
> ```
> int ledPin = 13;                  // LED connected to digital pin 13
>
> void setup()
> {
>   pinMode(ledPin, OUTPUT);        // sets the digital pin as output
> }
>
> void loop()
> {
>   digitalWrite(ledPin, HIGH);     // sets the LED on
>   delay(1000);                    // waits for a second
>   digitalWrite(ledPin, LOW);      // sets the LED off
>   delay(1000);                    // waits for a second
> }
> ```

Figure 22.1, digitalWrite docs

From the example code, this is pretty easy to use. Simply set the direction first, then write to the appropriate Arduino pin designator. Remember, the pin designators are the numbers written next to the headers on the Uno board, they're **not** the port bit numbers on the ATmega 328P! The reference note regarding Arduino pin 13 is worth re-reading. Pin 13 is hardwired to an on-board surface mount signaling LED located right next to said pin. This also means that the total source current available for pin 13 is somewhat reduced as LED current will also always be applied. Arduino pin 13 is PORTB bit 5 (sometimes written shorthand as PORTB.5).

So, just what does the `digitalWrite()` function do? Here is the code for `digitalWrite()`, slightly cleaned up for your viewing pleasure[19]:

---

[19] The original may be found in the file wiring_digital.c

Embedded Controllers

```
void digitalWrite( uint8_t pin, uint8_t val )
{
        uint8_t timer, bit, port, oldSREG;
        volatile uint8_t *out;

        timer = digitalPinToTimer( pin );
        bit =   digitalPinToBitMask( pin );
        port =  digitalPinToPort( pin );

        if (port == NOT_A_PIN) return;

        if (timer != NOT_ON_TIMER)    turnOffPWM( timer );

        out = portOutputRegister( port );

        oldSREG = SREG;
        cli();

        if (val == LOW)     *out &= ~bit;
        else                *out |= bit;

        SREG = oldSREG;
}
```

Figure 22.2, digitalWrite code

Let's take this apart, piece by piece, bit by bit. After the initial data declarations we see a group of function calls that serve to translate the Arduino pin designator into appropriate ATmega 328P ports, bits and timers. (The timer business we'll address shortly.) This section finishes with an error check. If the specified pin doesn't exist, the function bails out and does nothing.

```
        timer = digitalPinToTimer( pin );
        bit =   digitalPinToBitMask( pin );
        port =  digitalPinToPort( pin );

        if (port == NOT_A_PIN) return;
```

The AVR series of controllers, like most controllers, contain internal timers/counters. These allow the controller to precisely time events or produce pulse signals (specifically, pulse width modulation). The Arduino system pre-configures six of the available outputs with timers for use with the `analogWrite()` function. As not all pins have this ability, we need to translate the Arduino pin to an associated timer with the `digitalPinToTimer()` function. We will take a closer look at timers later, but for now it is only important to understand that any associated timer needs to be turned off before we can use our basic digital write function.

```
        if (timer != NOT_ON_TIMER)    turnOffPWM( timer );
```

The code to turn off the PWM functionality is little more than a `switch/case` statement. The `cbi()` call is used to clear a specific bit in a port, in this case the associated timer-counter control register (`TCCRx`). More info can be found at http://playground.arduino.cc/Main/AVR.

```
static void turnOffPWM( uint8_t timer )
{
    switch (timer)
    {
        case TIMER0A:   cbi(TCCR0A, COM0A1);    break;
        case TIMER0B:   cbi(TCCR0A, COM0B1);    break;
        case TIMER1A:   cbi(TCCR1A, COM1A1);    break;
        case TIMER1B:   cbi(TCCR1A, COM1B1);    break;
        case TIMER2A:   cbi(TCCR2A, COM2A1);    break;
        case TIMER2B:   cbi(TCCR2A, COM2B1);    break;
    }
}
```

After this, the specified Arduino port is translated to an output register, that is, PORTx.

```
out = portOutputRegister( port );
```

As was seen with pinMode(), the status register is saved, the global interrupt bit is cleared to disable all interrupts via the cli() call, the desired port (PORTx) is ANDed with the complement of the bit mask to clear it (i.e., set it low) or ORed with the bit mask to set it (i.e., set it high). The status register is then restored to its original state:

```
oldSREG = SREG;
cli();

if (val == LOW)   *out &= ~bit;
else              *out |= bit;

SREG = oldSREG;
```

That's pretty much it. Now, it you want to write a bunch of bits to a group of output port connections, you can simply look up the corresponding port for those Arduino pins (i.e., PORTx) and set or clear them directly. For example, if you want to clear bits 0, 1, and 4 of port B (i.e., 00010011 or 0x13), you could do the following (assuming no timer is active):

```
PORTB &= ~0x13;   // clear bits
```

or to set them:

```
PORTB |= 0x13;    // set bits
```

This would leave the other bits completely untouched. In contrast, suppose you want to set the bottom four bits (i.e., 0 through 3) to the binary pattern 0101. That's equivalent to 0x05. You could do the following:

```
PORTB = (PORTB & 0xf0)| 0x05;
```

The first chunk clears the bottom four bits and the trailing part sets the binary pattern. This would be preferable to clearing bits 1 and 3 and then setting bits 0 and 2 as that would cause two distinct sets of output voltage patterns at the external pins. Granted, the first set will exist for only a very short time but this can create problems in some applications.

23. Bits & Pieces: delay()

or How to Waste Time

Sometimes our code needs to wait for things or time events. For example, we might want to turn an LED on for a few seconds and then turn it off. We've seen how to control an LED with `digitalWrite()` but how do we wait for a few seconds? One simple method is to create an empty loop. This is a loop that really does nothing but waste time. For example, if we know that simply incrementing, testing and branching in a loop takes a microsecond, we could write a function like this:

```
void CheesyDelay( unsigned long msec )
{
  volatile unsigned long i;
  unsigned long endmsec = msec * 1000;

  for( i=0; i<endmsec; i++ );
}
```

Note that we specify the number of milliseconds we'd like to waste. Since each iteration of the loop takes one microsecond, we multiply by 1000 to achieve milliseconds. The `volatile` modifier is important here. This tells the compiler not to aggressively optimize the code for us because I could be changed by code running elsewhere (for example, in an interrupt). Otherwise, the compiler might figure out that it can achieve the same end result by ignoring the loop and doing a simple addition. The problem with this function is that the resulting delay is highly dependent on the microcontroller used and its clock frequency. If you just need a quick and dirty delay this will work fine, but a far more accurate delay is available with the `delay()` function and its sibling `delayMicroseconds()`, whose reference material is repeated below.

---

delay()[20]

Description

Pauses the program for the amount of time (in miliseconds) specified as parameter. (There are 1000 milliseconds in a second.)

Syntax

delay(ms)

Parameters

ms: the number of milliseconds to pause (*unsigned long*)

Returns

nothing

---

[20] http://arduino.cc/en/Reference/Delay

Example

```
int ledPin = 13;                    // LED connected to digital pin 13

void setup()
{
  pinMode(ledPin, OUTPUT);          // sets the digital pin as output
}

void loop()
{
  digitalWrite(ledPin, HIGH);   // sets the LED on
  delay(1000);                  // waits for a second
  digitalWrite(ledPin, LOW);    // sets the LED off
  delay(1000);                  // waits for a second
}
```

Caveat

While it is easy to create a blinking LED with the delay() function, and many sketches use short delays for such tasks as switch debouncing, the use of delay() in a sketch has significant drawbacks. No other reading of sensors, mathematical calculations, or pin manipulation can go on during the delay function, so in effect, it brings most other activity to a halt. For alternative approaches to controlling timing see the millis() function and the sketch sited below. More knowledgeable programmers usually avoid the use of delay() for timing of events longer than 10's of milliseconds unless the Arduino sketch is very simple.

Certain things *do* go on while the delay() function is controlling the Atmega chip however, because the delay function does not disable interrupts. Serial communication that appears at the RX pin is recorded, PWM (analogWrite) values and pin states are maintained, and interrupts will work as they should.

See also

- millis()
- micros()
- delayMicroseconds()
- Blink Without Delay example

delayMicroseconds()

Description

Pauses the program for the amount of time (in microseconds) specified as parameter. There are a thousand microseconds in a millisecond, and a million microseconds in a second.

Currently, the largest value that will produce an accurate delay is 16383. This could change in future Arduino releases. For delays longer than a few thousand microseconds, you should use delay() instead.

> Syntax
>
> delayMicroseconds(us)
>
> Parameters
>
> us: the number of microseconds to pause (*unsigned int*)
>
> Returns
>
> None
>
> Caveats and Known Issues
>
> This function works very accurately in the range 3 microseconds and up. We cannot assure that delayMicroseconds will perform precisely for smaller delay-times.
>
> As of Arduino 0018, delayMicroseconds() no longer disables interrupts.

Figure 23.1, delay docs

These functions are also tied in with two other functions, micros() and millis(), which are repeated below:

> **millis()**
>
> Description
>
> Returns the number of milliseconds since the Arduino board began running the current program. This number will overflow (go back to zero), after approximately 50 days.
>
> Parameters
>
> None
>
> Returns
>
> Number of milliseconds since the program started (*unsigned long*)
>
> Tip:
>
> Note that the parameter for millis is an unsigned long, errors may be generated if a programmer tries to do math with other datatypes such as ints

> ### micros()
>
> Description
>
> Returns the number of microseconds since the Arduino board began running the current program. This number will overflow (go back to zero), after approximately 70 minutes. On 16 MHz Arduino boards (e.g. Duemilanove and Nano), this function has a resolution of four microseconds (i.e. the value returned is always a multiple of four). On 8 MHz Arduino boards (e.g. the LilyPad), this function has a resolution of eight microseconds.
>
> Parameters
>
> None
>
> Returns
>
> Number of microseconds since the program started (*unsigned long*)

Figure 23.2, millis and micros docs

All of these functions rely on the Arduino system configuring the timers the moment the board is reset. One of these will be used to generate an interrupt when the counter overflows. The time to overflow will take a predetermined amount of time based on the clock speed. The interrupt will in turn update three global variables that will keep track of how long the program has been running.

First let's consider the initialization code along with some definitions and global variable declarations. Besides this timer, the init code also sets up the other timers for pulse width modulation duties (via the `analogWrite()` function). The code is reasonably well commented and is presented without further explanation, save for a reminder that `sbi()` is a macro that will reduce to a single assembly language instruction that sets a specific register bit.

```
#include "wiring_private.h"

// the prescaler is set so that timer0 ticks every 64 clock cycles, and the
// the overflow handler is called every 256 ticks.
#define MICROSECONDS_PER_TIMER0_OVERFLOW (clockCyclesToMicroseconds(64 * 256))

// the whole number of milliseconds per timer0 overflow
#define MILLIS_INC (MICROSECONDS_PER_TIMER0_OVERFLOW / 1000)

// the fractional number of milliseconds per timer0 overflow. we shift right
// by three to fit these numbers into a byte. (for the clock speeds we care
// about - 8 and 16 MHz - this doesn't lose precision.)
#define FRACT_INC ((MICROSECONDS_PER_TIMER0_OVERFLOW % 1000) >> 3)
#define FRACT_MAX (1000 >> 3)

volatile unsigned long timer0_overflow_count = 0;
volatile unsigned long timer0_millis = 0;
static unsigned char timer0_fract = 0;
```

Embedded Controllers

```c
void init()
{
    // this needs to be called before setup() or some functions won't
    // work there
    sei();

    // set timer 0 prescale factor to 64
    sbi(TCCR0B, CS01);
    sbi(TCCR0B, CS00);

    // enable timer 0 overflow interrupt
    sbi(TIMSK0, TOIE0);

    // timers 1 and 2 are used for phase-correct hardware pwm
    // this is better for motors as it ensures an even waveform
    // note, however, that fast pwm mode can achieve a frequency of up
    // 8 MHz (with a 16 MHz clock) at 50% duty cycle

    TCCR1B = 0;

    // set timer 1 prescale factor to 64
    sbi(TCCR1B, CS11);
    sbi(TCCR1B, CS10);

    // put timer 1 in 8-bit phase correct pwm mode
    sbi(TCCR1A, WGM10);

    // set timer 2 prescale factor to 64
    sbi(TCCR2B, CS22);

    // configure timer 2 for phase correct pwm (8-bit)
    sbi(TCCR2A, WGM20);


    // set a2d prescale factor to 128
    // 16 MHz / 128 = 125 KHz, inside the desired 50-200 KHz range.
    // XXX: this will not work properly for other clock speeds, and
    // this code should use F_CPU to determine the prescale factor.
    sbi(ADCSRA, ADPS2);
    sbi(ADCSRA, ADPS1);
    sbi(ADCSRA, ADPS0);

    // enable a2d conversions
    sbi(ADCSRA, ADEN);

    // the bootloader connects pins 0 and 1 to the USART; disconnect
    // them here so they can be used as normal digital i/o;
    // they will be reconnected in Serial.begin()
    UCSR0B = 0;
}
```

Figure 23.3, timer setup code

Now let's take a look at the interrupt service routine. Each time the counter overflows (i.e. the 8 bit counter tries to increment 255 and wraps back to 0) it generates an interrupt which calls this function. Basically, all it does is increment the global variables declared earlier.

```c
SIGNAL( TIMER0_OVF_vect )
{
    // copy these to local variables so they can be stored in
    // registers (volatile vars are read from memory on every access)
    unsigned long m = timer0_millis;
    unsigned char f = timer0_fract;

    m += MILLIS_INC;
    f += FRACT_INC;

    if (f >= FRACT_MAX)
    {
        f -= FRACT_MAX;
        m += 1;
    }

    timer0_fract = f;
    timer0_millis = m;
    timer0_overflow_count++;
}
```

Figure 23.4, timer interrupt code

As you might now guess, all the `millis()` and `micros()` functions do is access these global variables and return their values. Because an interrupt can occur during this process, the value of the status register (SREG) is copied, the status register's global interrupt enable bit is cleared with the `cli()` call, the access performed (plus a little extra calculation for `micros()`) and the status register returned to its prior state. The retrieved value is then returned to the caller.

```c
unsigned long millis()
{
    unsigned long m;
    uint8_t oldSREG = SREG;

    // disable interrupts while we read timer0_millis or we might get
    // an inconsistent value (e.g. in the middle of a write to
    // timer0_millis)

    cli();
    m = timer0_millis;
    SREG = oldSREG;

    return m;
}
```

```
unsigned long micros()
{
    unsigned long m;
    uint8_t t, oldSREG = SREG;

    cli();
    m = timer0_overflow_count;
    t = TCNT0;
    if ((TIFR0 & _BV(TOV0)) && (t < 255))      m++;
    SREG = oldSREG;

    return ((m << 8) + t) * (64 / clockCyclesPerMicrosecond());
}
```

Figure 23.5, millis and micros code

So the `delay()` function itself is pretty straightforward. It simply retrieves the current time since reset and then goes into a "busy wait" loop, constantly checking and rechecking the time until the difference between the two reaches the requested value.

```
void delay(unsigned long ms)
{
    uint16_t start;

    start = (uint16_t)micros();

    while (ms > 0)
    {
        if (((uint16_t)micros() - start) >= 1000)
        {
            ms--;
            start += 1000;
        }
    }
}
```

Figure 23.6, delay code

In a way, this is just a slightly more sophisticated version of our initial cheesy delay function. It is more precise because it uses the accurate internal counters which are operating from a known clock frequency. The microseconds version of the delay is a little trickier, especially for short delays. This also does a busy wait but does so using in-line assembly code. Even with this, the delays are not particularly accurate for periods of only a few microseconds. In the in-line comments are instructive:

```
/* Delay in microseconds. Assumes 8 or 16 MHz clock. */

void delayMicroseconds(unsigned int us)
{
        // for the 16 MHz clock on most Arduino boards
        // for a one-microsecond delay, simply return.  the overhead
        // of the function call yields a delay of approximately 1 1/8 us.
        if (--us == 0)
              return;

        // the following loop takes a quarter of a microsecond (4 cycles)
        // per iteration, so execute it four times for each microsecond of
        // delay requested.
        us <<= 2;

        // account for the time taken in the preceding commands.
        us -= 2;

        // busy wait
        __asm__ __volatile__ (
              "1: sbiw %0,1" "\n\t" // 2 cycles
              "brne 1b" : "=w" (us) : "0" (us) // 2 cycles
        );
}
```

Figure 23.7, delayMicroseconds code

The major problem with using `delay()` is noted in its on-line documentation, namely, that during a busy wait loop no other work can be done. The controller is effectively "spinning its wheels". A more effective way to delay is to make direct use of the `millis()` function. The basic idea is to check the time using `millis()` and then do what you need to do inside a loop, checking the elapsed time on each iteration. Here is a snippet of example code.

```
unsigned long currentMillis, previousMillis, intervalToWait;

// intervalToWait could be a passed variable, global or define

// initialize to current time
previousMillis = millis();
currentMillis = millis();

while ( currentMillis - previousMillis < intervalToWait )
{
    // do whatever you need to do here

    currentMillis = millis();
}
```

In essence you've built your own "kind of" busy wait loop but with requisite code inside.

Embedded Controllers

24. Bits & Pieces: digitalRead()

24.1 Introduction

The discussion that follows deals strictly with two-state high/low logic level sensing. For continuously variable analog signals see the Bits & Pieces entry covering `analogRead()`. Through the `pinMode()` function, or by directly accessing the appropriate data direction register bits (`DDRx`), the general purpose IO connections can be configured to read the state of external switches or logic levels. With the Arduino Uno, 5 volts represents a logic high while 0 volts represents a logic low. An added capacity of the ATmega 328P on the Uno is the ability to include an optional internal pull-up resistor at the input pin. This allows connection of a simple passive short-to-ground switch (i.e. the input pin floats high when the switch is open and goes low when the switch is engaged).

To read individual pin inputs the Arduino system offers the `digitalRead()` function. Multiple pins can be read simultaneously by directly accessing the appropriate register, which we will examine afterward. Below is a copy of the online documentation for the `digitalRead()` function:

---

digitalRead()[21]

Description

Reads the value from a specified digital pin, either HIGH or LOW.

Syntax

digitalRead(pin)

Parameters

pin: the number of the digital pin you want to read (*int*)

Returns

HIGH or LOW

Example
```
int ledPin = 13;  // LED connected to digital pin 13
int inPin = 7;    // pushbutton connected to digital pin 7
int val = 0;      // variable to store the read value

void setup()
{
  pinMode(ledPin, OUTPUT);   // sets the digital pin 13 as output
  pinMode(inPin, INPUT);     // sets the digital pin 7 as input
}
void loop()
{
  val = digitalRead(inPin);     // read the input pin
  digitalWrite(ledPin, val);    // sets the LED to the button's value
}
```

---

[21] http://arduino.cc/en/Reference/DigitalRead

> Sets pin 13 to the same value as the pin 7, which is an input.
>
> Note
>
> If the pin isn't connected to anything, digitalRead() can return either HIGH or LOW (and this can change randomly).
>
> The analog input pins can be used as digital pins, referred to as A0, A1, etc.
>
> See also
>
> - pinMode()
>
> - digitalWrite()
>
> - Tutorial: Digital Pins

Figure 24.1, digitalRead docs

A slightly cleaned-up version of the source code follows (found in the file wiring_digital.c):

```
int digitalRead( uint8_t pin )
{
    uint8_t timer, bit, port;

    timer = digitalPinToTimer( pin );
    bit =   digitalPinToBitMask( pin );
    port =  digitalPinToPort( pin );

    if (port == NOT_A_PIN)              return LOW;

    if (timer != NOT_ON_TIMER)          turnOffPWM(timer);

    if (*portInputRegister(port) & bit) return HIGH;

    return LOW;
}
static void turnOffPWM( uint8_t timer )
{
    switch ( timer )
    {
        case TIMER0A:   cbi( TCCR0A, COM0A1 );   break;
        case TIMER0B:   cbi( TCCR0A, COM0B1 );   break;

        // and so forth for all available timers, not shown
    }
}
```

Figure 24.2, digitalRead code

Embedded Controllers

The first three lines convert the Arduino pin designator to the appropriate ATmega 328P port, bit number and timer. If the port is invalid, the function exits.

```
timer = digitalPinToTimer( pin );
bit   = digitalPinToBitMask( pin );
port  = digitalPinToPort( pin );

if (port == NOT_A_PIN)                    return LOW;
```

The timer is important because the Arduino system preconfigures the Uno's three on-board timers for use with the `analogWrite()` function through a pulse width modulation scheme. This affects six of the possible pins. For proper operation of the digital read, these timers need to be turned off. We saw this same bit of code inside the `digitalWrite()` function.

```
if (timer != NOT_ON_TIMER)                turnOffPWM(timer);
```

At this point the contents of the input register are read (the direct name of the input register is `PINx`) and then ANDed with the requested bit. This removes all of the other bits so we can return either a simple high or low.

```
if (*portInputRegister(port) & bit) return HIGH;

return LOW;
```

The function used to turn off the pulse width modulation timers is little more than a `switch/case` statement. If the specified Arduino pin is hooked up to a timer internally, that timer is found in the switch statement and a `cbi()` call is executed on the appropriate timer-counter control register. The `cbi()` function translates to a single assembly language instruction to clear the specified bit in the control register, thus turning off that timer.

```
static void turnOffPWM( uint8_t timer )
{
    switch (timer)
    {
        case TIMER0A:     cbi(TCCR0A, COM0A1);    break;
        case TIMER0B:     cbi(TCCR0A, COM0B1);    break;
        case TIMER1A:     cbi(TCCR1A, COM1A1);    break;
        case TIMER1B:     cbi(TCCR1A, COM1B1);    break;
        case TIMER2A:     cbi(TCCR2A, COM2A1);    break;
        case TIMER2B:     cbi(TCCR2A, COM2B1);    break;
    }
}
```

In some applications, several bits need to be read at once, for example when reading parallel data. This can be performed through a direct access of the appropriate `PINx` register. `PINx` is rather like the fraternal twin of the `PORTx` register. While `PORTx` is used to write digital data to an external connection, `PINx` is where you read digital data from an external connection. Just as there are four output port registers, A through D, there are four input pin registers, A through D. Not all microcontrollers are configured this way. Some of them use the same register for both reading and writing (the function being controlled by the associated data direction register).

Here is how to directly access a single bit on a non-timer connected pin. First, clear the desired data direction register bit to activate input mode. Second, if desired, set the same bit in the associated port register to enable the optional pull-up resistor. If you don't want the pull-up, leave that bit clear. Finally, read the desired bit in the pin register and AND it with the bit mask to remove the other bits. For example, to read bit 4 (0x10 or 00010000 in binary) on port B:

```
DDRB  &= (~0x10);       // activate input mode
PORTB |= 0x10;          // enable pull-up or use the bitSet macro
                        // bitSet( PORTB, 4 );
value = PINB & 0x10;    // retrieve data
```

It is only minor work to alter this for multiple bits. To read both bits 0 and 4 but without the pull-up resistors (bit pattern 00010001 or 0x11):

```
DDRB  &= (~0x11);       // activate input mode
PORTB &= (~0x11);       // disable pull-up
value = PINB & 0x11;    // retrieve data bits
```

or if you want the bits separately:

```
value0 = PINB & 0x01;   // retrieve data bit 0
value4 = PINB & 0x10;   // retrieve data bit 4
```

24.2 A Practical Example: Round-Robin Switch

Let's take a look at how we might implement a *round-robin* switch. A round-robin switch works in a circular manner; stepping through a sequence of settings and returning back to the start once the sequence is completed. For our example, we shall consider a single momentary contact pushbutton that cycles through a series of fan speeds: off, low, medium and high. The system will start in the off state and each successive press of the button will advance the state from low through high. Once high is reached, a further press will cycle the state back to off and the process continues in like manner. Each speed setting will be indicated via its own LED and only one LED will be on at any given time. To keep the code clean, will only examine the pushbutton and LED portion of the code and not consider how we might control the speed of a fan. Further, we shall assume that an appropriate hardware debounce circuit is incorporated with the pushbutton (e.g., a 74HC14 Schmitt with RC network) and that depressing the button will produce a logical high at our Arduino input pin. Also, the LED drivers are assumed to be active high (i.e., a high on an output pin of the Arduino will light an LED).

The first thing to remember is that a typical microcontroller is capable of checking the state of an input pin in a fraction of a microsecond. Consequently, we cannot simply check the pin to see if it is a logical high, and if so, cycle through to the next fan speed. In the fraction of a second it would take for a human to press and release the button, the microcontroller could loop through the pin checking code thousands of times, cycling the fan speed for each loop's check. The final fan speed would be anyone's guess. Instead, we need to look for the low to high transition as this happens only once with each button press. Indeed, this also points up the need for switch debouncing. Without it, a single press could result in over a dozen low to high edges due to switch contact chatter resulting in a random fan setting. One way to perform the positive going edge detection is to use two variables, one for the current state of the switch and a second for the prior state of the switch (i.e., the state that was measured immediately prior to the current state). If the current state is high (on or pressed) and the prior state is low (off or not pressed) then we know we have detected a positive going edge and we can perform our processing. Note that on the next iteration of the loop, the current state will be high but the prior state will now also be high (i.e., the former current state from the prior loop iteration) and thus no processing is performed. At this point it would not matter how long the user kept their finger on the button as all current and prior states will be high. When the user finally releases the button the current state will be low with a prior state of high. This is the negative going edge and, again, we have no need to process it. The next loop iteration will produce current and prior states of low with no need to process. Eventually, when the user presses the button again we'll see a current state of high with a prior state of low and we'll process this edge.

We'll need three variables for the states, namely the current and prior pushbutton states and another for the LEDs (which indicate fan speed). The pushbuttons can be thought of as Boolean variables (0/1) while the LED variable will range from 0 through 3, 0 being "off" and 3 being "high". For simplicity, we'll use globals for these, `unsigned char`s will do nicely. The four LEDs will be positioned off of Arduino Uno pins 8 through 11 (PORTB.0:3) and the pushbutton will be connected to pin 12 (PORTB.4). The `setup()` function will have to set the proper directions for these port bits. This would require five separate calls to `pinMode()` but only two simple operations if we operate directly. Here is the beginning portion:

```
// declare the state variables and initialize at 0 for "off"
unsigned char currentstate=0;
unsigned char priorstate=0;
unsigned char ledstate=0;

// define some values for the LED/fan state. These are conveniently
// chosen to be the FAN/LED bit positions in PORTB
#define FAN_OFF    0
#define FAN_LO     1
#define FAN_MED    2
#define FAN_HIGH   3

// declare bit masks for the four LED bits and pushbutton
#define LED_OFF    0x01
#define LED_LOW    0x02
#define LED_MED    0x04
#define LED_HIGH   0x08
#define PBUTTON    0x10

// the LED_XXX masks could also be defined like so:
// #define LED_OFF (1<<FAN_OFF)

// a convenience
#define LED_ALL    (LED_OFF|LED_LOW|LED_MED|LED_HIGH)


setup()
{
    // set for output
    DDRB |= LED_ALL;
    // set for input
    DDRB &= ~PBUTTON;

    // light up the "off" LED
    PORTB |= LED_OFF;
    // by default, outputs are 0 but if for some reason the other
    // LEDs could be on, be sure to set them to off before continuing
    // PORTB &= ~(LED_LOW|LED_MED|LED_HIGH);
}
```

The looping code needs to check for the proper current state/prior state pair. If it is not found, there is nothing to do. If it is found, we need to turn off the existing LED and then check the current LED/fan state, increment to the next state and light that LED. There are a couple ways to do this. The first is perhaps an obvious solution using a switch/case construct. The second method is a bit more compact (pun intended).

```
loop()
{
    // get current button state
    currentstate = PINB & PBUTTON;

    // do we have a positive going edge?
    if( currentstate && !priorstate )
    {
        switch( ledstate )
        {
            case FAN_OFF:
                PORTB &= ~LED_OFF;   // turn off old LED
                PORTB |= LED_LOW;    // turn on new LED
                ledstate = FAN_LOW;  // increment speed
                break;

            case FAN_LOW:
                PORTB &= ~LED_LOW;
                PORTB |= LED_MED;
                ledstate = FAN_MED;
                break;

            case FAN_MED:
                PORTB &= ~LED_MED;
                PORTB |= LED_HIGH;
                ledstate = FAN_HIGH;
                break;

            case FAN_HIGH:
                PORTB &= ~LED_HIGH;
                PORTB |= LED_OFF;
                ledstate = FAN_OFF;
                break;
        }
    }

    // update state for next loop iteration
    priorstate = currentstate;
}
```

The alternate version can be found on the next page. Note the code savings. Instead of checking for each fan state, we turn off all LEDs and increment the fan state. If the state would increment past the maximum then we make sure to set it to the off state. This new state tells us which LED to light. This version works with little code because of the way in which we chose our bit positions. This is not always possible (or even desirable) but can be a handy technique from time to time.

Embedded Controllers

```
loop()
{
      // get current button state
      currentstate = PINB & PBUTTON;

      // do we have a positive going edge?
      if( currentstate && !priorstate )
      {
            // increment to new state
            if( ledstate < FAN_HIGH )
                  ledstate++;
            else
                  ledstate = FAN_OFF;

            // lazy: turn off all LEDs
            PORTB &= ~LED_ALL;
            // turn on new LED
            PORTB |= (1<<ledstate);
      }

      // update state for next loop iteration
      priorstate = currentstate;
}
```

24.3 Exercise

In closing, here's an interesting question. If the round-robin switch had numerous states, say a dozen or so, a single increment button might prove a little frustrating to the user. For example, if they accidentally go past the desired setting then they're forced to go all the way around again to effectively "back up". To alleviate this we could add a decrement pushbutton alongside our existing increment pushbutton. How would the code example presented above need to be altered to respond to a two button configuration? If at first this appears to be too daunting of a challenge, then break it into two parts. Initially, consider how the preceding code would need to be altered in order to change the operation of the fan speed increment button into a fan speed decrement button. That is, instead of button pushes producing the sequence *off-low-med-high-off* etc., implement the button to produce *off-high-med-low-off* etc. Once this is completed, determine how to combine this new implementation with the existing example code.

http://xkcd.com/156/

25. Bits & Pieces: Analog Input Circuitry

25.1 Introduction

As useful as digital input/output ports are, there is also a need for continuously variable or analog ports. Controllers are, of course, inherently digital devices but that doesn't mean that analog signals are out of bounds. There is considerable variation in what is available on any given microcontroller, though. On some units, analog to digital and digital to analog circuitry must be added to the controller system as peripheral devices. This is particularly true for less expensive controllers or for more specialized applications that require extreme performance (for example, a high definition digital audio recorder or playback device). Most general purpose controllers have an analog to digital converter (ADC) and some also include a digital to analog converter (DAC). The resolution and speed of these converters can vary quite a bit from controller to controller. In this chapter we shall focus on the ADC system found in the ATmega series. While our discussion will be quite specific, the concepts presented apply to many other controllers made by other manufacturers. Only the performance and operational details may differ.

A typical use of an ADC is to capture the value of an external sensor or user input device at a particular point in time. For instance, we may wish to measure the output voltage from a temperature or light sensor. Regarding a user interface device, one possibility is to measure the voltage developed across a potentiometer (the outer terminals connected to power and ground, the wiper attached to the analog input port). As the user rotates the pot, the voltage shifts. This voltage could represent all manner of variables from the loudness setting for music playback to the speed of a motor. These sorts of applications can be considered "snapshot" or single conversion uses. That is, we don't spend all of our time continuously converting the port voltage to digital values the way we would with, say, a waveform capture device. In the case of something like a temperature sensor, we simply perform conversions as we need them. For user interface devices, as long as we can obtain values at a sufficiently fast rate, the control will appear continuous to the user. In some applications this may require no more than a dozen or so conversions per second. This is compared to tens of thousands of conversions per second for something like digitizing audio signals.

Of course, we may need to have several user interface devices. Consider something as common as a stereo receiver. Typically we would find knobs for volume, balance, bass, treble and so forth. It would be very impractical to have a single knob that controls everything and a series of buttons alongside it to indicate the current function of the knob. Alternately, in an industrial setting we might need to monitor temperatures at several locations along with other environmental parameters. While we could use one ADC for each of these, it makes far more sense to use a single ADC and multiplex it to several external pins. Think of these as multiple input channels. We select the channel (sensor) we want, make the measurement and continue on.

This is not to say that we only use this "snapshot" mode. There are other applications that require continuous monitoring of the external signal and other techniques of obtaining the measurement. Consequently, ADC systems can be configured for a single on-demand conversion as above, they can be free-running or the conversion can be triggered by some other event. Because of these demands, the circuitry and programming interface for analog inputs tends to be much more involved (and much more flexible) than we've seen for digital inputs. For example, ADC systems often have several registers and bits devoted to specifying parameters such as the sample acquisition mode, the conversion speed, data justification, pin muxing and so forth.

25.2 ATmega ADC system

A block diagram of the ATmega ADC system is found in Figure 25.1.

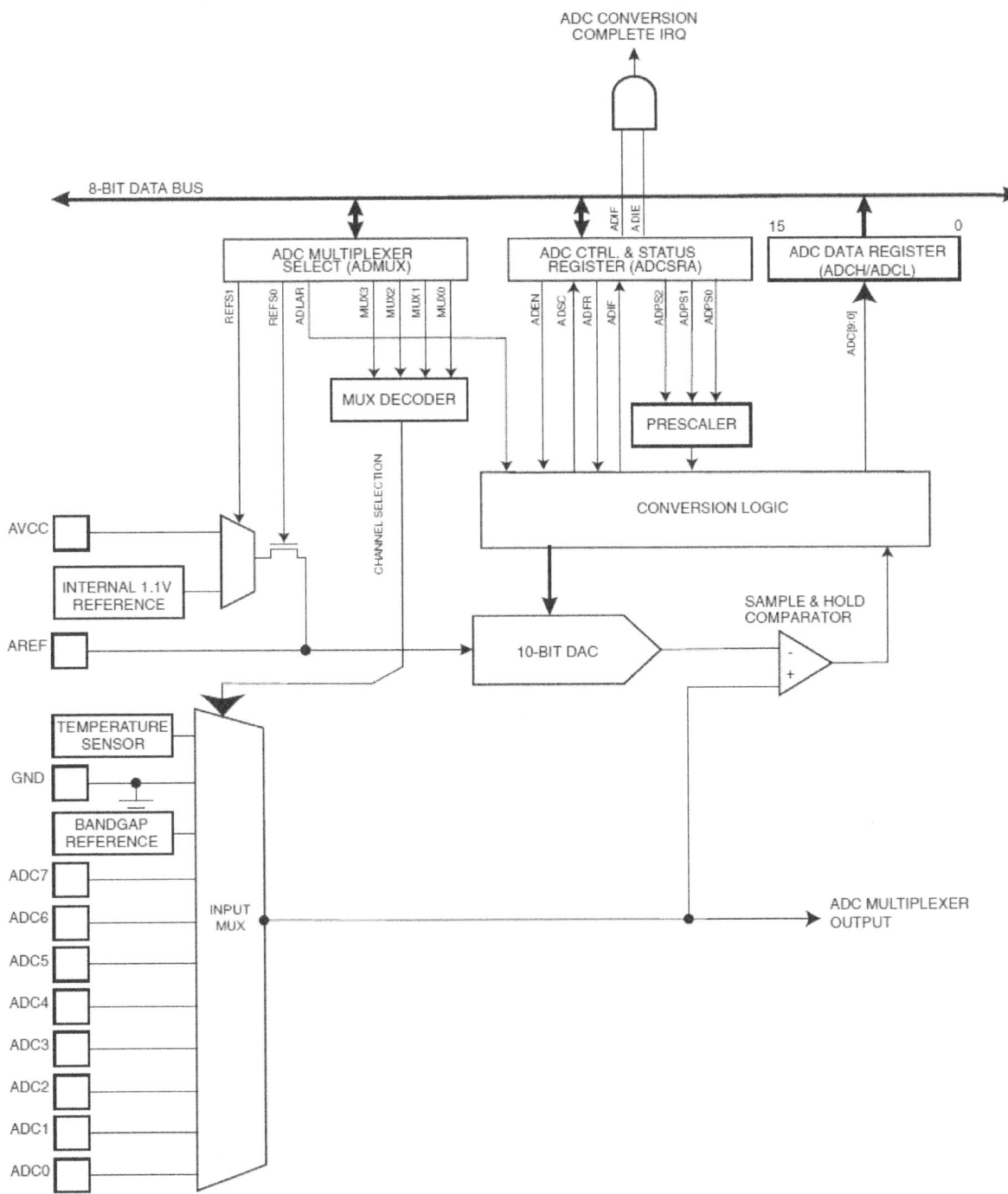

Figure 25.1, ADC circuitry (Atmel 2014)

Embedded Controllers

The heart of the system is a single successive approximation DAC with 10 bit resolution. Maximum conversion speed at full resolution is about 15 k samples per second. Clearly this is insufficient for applications such as CD quality audio or video but is more than fast enough for most sensor and user interface monitoring. The converter performance specifications include 0.5 LSB integral non-linearity error and ±2 LSB absolute accuracy. An on-board reference is available although an external reference may also be used. The converter includes a sample-and-hold system to stabilize the measurement for rapidly changing input signals. There is an eight channel mux although only six of these channels are used on some packages (the package used on the standard configuration of the Arduino Uno board uses six). The input circuitry is optimized for sources that have an output impedance of 10 KΩ or less. It is also very important to recognize that the system is unipolar and will only respond to positive voltages. If the signal to be measured is bipolar, some manner of DC level shifting will be required.

There are several registers associated with the ADC system. These are shown in Figure 25.2.

Register	Bit 7	Bit 6	Bit 5	Bit 4	Bit 3	Bit 2	Bit 1	Bit 0
ADCSRA	ADEN	ADSC	ADATE	ADIF	ADIE	ADPS2	ADPS1	ADPS0
ADCSRB	-	ACME	-	-	-	ADTS2	ADTS1	ADTS0
ADMUX	REFS1	REFS0	ADLAR	-	MUX3	MUX2	MUX1	MUX0
ADCH	ADC9/-	ADC8/-	ADC7/-	ADC6/-	ADC5/-	ADC4/-	ADC3/9	ADC2/8
ADCL	ADC1/7	ADC0/6	-/ADC5	-/ADC4	-/ADC3	-/ADC2	-/ADC1	-/ADC0

Figure 26.2, ADC registers

ADCSRA and ADCSRB are the Analog-Digital Control and Status Registers. Here are their bit descriptions:

- ADEN: ENable. Set to one to enable to Analog-Digital system.
- ADSC : Start Conversion. Set to one to start a conversion. When the conversion is complete, the hardware will reset this bit to zero. Writing zero to this bit will have no effect.
- ADATE: Auto Trigger Enable. Set to one for auto trigger mode. A rising edge on the selected trigger signal will start a conversion. The trigger source is selected via the ADTS bits in the ADCSRB register (below).
- ADIF: Interrupt Flag. This is used with interrupt mode. This bit is set when a conversion is complete and the data registers are updated. This bit is cleared by the hardware when executing the interrupt handler routine. Use with ADIE.
- ADIE: Interrupt Enabled. Set to one to enable the ADC conversion interrupt. Use with ADIF.
- ADPS2-0: Prescaler bits. These bits are used to divide down the system clock to the ADC clock. 000 and 001 yield division by two and increasing values double the clock divide with 111 yielding divide by 128.
- ACME: Analog Comparator Multiplexer Enabled. Setting these bits allows any of the eight multiplexed ADC pins to replace the negative input to the analog comparator.
- ADTS2-0: Trigger Source. If ADATE is set to one, these bits determine the trigger source. 000 is free running mode, 001 triggers from the analog comparator, 010 uses External Interrupt Request 0, and the remaining values set various timer/counter sources.

`ADMUX` is the Analog-Digital MUltipleXer selection register. It is also used for reference selection and data justification. The bit descriptions follow:

- `REFS1-0`: REFerence voltages. 00 yields the `AREF` pin, 01 yields `AVCC`, 11 yields internal 1.1 volt reference and 10 is reserved.
- `ADLAR`: Left Adjust Result. Setting this bit will left justify the output bits in the `ADCH`/`ADCL` registers. Setting to zero right justifies.
- `MUX3-0`: MUltipleXer. These bits select the input pin. 000 selects `ADC0`, 001 selects `ADC1` and so on to 1000 selecting `ADC8` (the temperature sensor). 1110 selects the 1.1 volt reference and 1111 selects ground. All other values are reserved.

Finally we have `ADCH` and `ADCL`, the ADC High and Low output registers. There are two registers because this is a 10 bit converter but the registers only hold eight bits each. There are two modes of operation in conjunction with the `ADLAR` bit in the `ADMUX` register. If `ADLAR` is set then the top eight bits will be placed into `ADCH` and the bottom two bits will be placed at the top of `ADCL`. If `ADLAR` is cleared then the bottom eight bits will be found in `ADCL` and the top two bits will be found at the bottom of `ADCH`. Just think of the two registers as a single 16 bit register with the bits pushed to the left or right as shown in Figure 26.3.

ADLAR	ADCH								ADCL							
	Bit 15	Bit 14	Bit 13	Bit 12	Bit 11	Bit 10	Bit 9	Bit 8	Bit 7	Bit 6	Bit 5	Bit 4	Bit 3	Bit 2	Bit 1	Bit 0
1	ADC 9	ADC 8	ADC 7	ADC 6	ADC 5	ADC 4	ADC 3	ADC 2	ADC 1	ADC 0	-	-	-	-	-	-
0	-	-	-	-	-	-	ADC 9	ADC 8	ADC 7	ADC 6	ADC 5	ADC 4	ADC 3	ADC 2	ADC 1	ADC 0

Figure 26.3, data justification

If only eight bits of resolution are needed, it is possible to left justify and read just `ADCH`, ignoring `ADCL`.

Single conversion operation is fairly straightforward. First, set up your initialization section. This begins with setting `ADEN` to enable the system. Then decide on the proper prescale value. The chip specifications indicate that the successive approximation circuitry will perform best with an ADC clock in the range of 50 kHz to 200 kHz. A typical conversion will take 13 ADC clock cycles (the first conversion will take 25 due to initialization overhead). Once this is determined, set `ADLAR` for data justification and `REFS` for the reference voltage. Then set the `ADMUX` bits to determine the input channel. Finally, set `ADSC` to start a conversion. You can wait on this bit or come back to it later. When the conversion is complete the hardware will reset it to zero. At that point read the value from `ADCL` and combine (shift and OR) with the value read from `ADCH` into a 16 bit integer. Note that you *must* read `ADCL` before reading `ADCH`. Reading `ADCL` locks the ADC registers preventing the hardware from overwriting the registers on a subsequent conversion. Reading `ADCH` unlocks them.

We will take a closer look at the software process in the next chapter.

26. Bits & Pieces: analogRead()

26.1 Introduction

Just as we would like to read the state of simple on/off switches, we also need to read continuously variable (i.e. analog) data. Usually this means the output voltage caused by some form of sensor such as a temperature sensor, force sensor, light sensor, etc. Very often simple passive devices such as CdS cells or FSRs are placed into a resistive bridge network, the output voltage of which will shift with changes in the environment. An even simpler application would be the use of a potentiometer hooked up to a fixed voltage supply. The position of the pot would be controlled by the user and could represent a setting of almost any conceivable parameter such as volume, brightness, time delay, frequency, etc. In order to read analog quantities, the ATmega 328P contains a single 10 bit analog-to-digital converter multiplexed across six input channels. On the Arduino Uno board, the inputs to these ADCs are found at the pins labeled A0 through A5. The Arduino development environment contains two useful functions to access theses, namely `analogRead()` and `analogReference()`. The on-line function descriptions are repeated below:

---

analogRead()[22]

Description

Reads the value from the specified analog pin. The Arduino board contains a 6 channel (8 channels on the Mini and Nano, 16 on the Mega), 10-bit analog to digital converter. This means that it will map input voltages between 0 and 5 volts into integer values between 0 and 1023. This yields a resolution between readings of: 5 volts / 1024 units or, 0.0049 volts (4.9 mV) per unit. The input range and resolution can be changed using analogReference().

It takes about 100 microseconds (0.0001 s) to read an analog input, so the maximum reading rate is about 10,000 times a second.

Syntax

analogRead(pin)

Parameters

pin: the number of the analog input pin to read from (0 to 5 on most boards, 0 to 7 on the Mini and Nano, 0 to 15 on the Mega)

Returns

int (0 to 1023)

Note

If the analog input pin is not connected to anything, the value returned by analogRead() will fluctuate based on a number of factors (e.g. the values of the other analog inputs, how close your hand is to the board, etc.).

---

[22] http://arduino.cc/en/Reference/AnalogRead

See also

- analogReference()

- Tutorial: Analog Input Pins

analogReference()[23]

Description

Configures the reference voltage used for analog input (i.e. the value used as the top of the input range). The options are:

- DEFAULT: the default analog reference of 5 volts (on 5V Arduino boards) or 3.3 volts (on 3.3V Arduino boards)

- INTERNAL: an built-in reference, equal to 1.1 volts on the ATmega168 or ATmega328 and 2.56 volts on the ATmega8 (*not available on the Arduino Mega*)

- INTERNAL1V1: a built-in 1.1V reference (*Arduino Mega only*)

- INTERNAL2V56: a built-in 2.56V reference (*Arduino Mega only*)

- EXTERNAL: the voltage applied to the AREF pin (**0 to 5V only**) is used as the reference.

Syntax

analogReference(type)

Parameters

type: which type of reference to use (DEFAULT, INTERNAL, INTERNAL1V1, INTERNAL2V56, or EXTERNAL).

Returns

None.

Note

After changing the analog reference, the first few readings from analogRead() may not be accurate.

Warning

Don't use anything less than 0V or more than 5V for external reference voltage on the AREF pin! If you're using an external reference on the AREF pin, you must set the analog reference to EXTERNAL before calling analogRead(). Otherwise, you will short together the active reference voltage (internally generated) and the AREF pin, possibly damaging the microcontroller on your Arduino board.

Alternatively, you can connect the external reference voltage to the AREF pin through a 5K resistor,

---

[23] http://arduino.cc/en/Reference/AnalogReference

> allowing you to switch between external and internal reference voltages. Note that the resistor will alter the voltage that gets used as the reference because there is an internal 32K resistor on the AREF pin. The two act as a voltage divider, so, for example, 2.5V applied through the resistor will yield 2.5 * 32 / (32+5) = ~2.2V at the AREF pin.
>
> See also
>
> - Description of the analog input pins
> - analogRead()

Figure 26.1, analogRead and analogReference docs

The `analogRead()` function is best used as a single conversion "snapshot". This is good for simple user interface and basic sensor applications. Generally speaking, `analogReference()` is called once during the setup and initialization phase of the program. Also, unless there is a compelling reason to do otherwise, the default mode is the best place to start. This will yield a 5 volt peak to peak input range with a bit resolution of just under 4.9 millivolts (5/1024). **It is important to note that this range runs from 0 volts to 5 volts, not −2.5 volts to +2.5 volts.** Depending on the amplitude and frequency range of the sensor signal, some input processing circuitry may be required to apply a DC offset, amplify or reduce signal strength, filter frequency extremes and so forth.

The code for `analogReference()` is about as simple as it gets. It just sets (and hides) a global variable which will be accessed by the `analogRead()` function:

```
uint8_t analog_reference = DEFAULT;

void analogReference(uint8_t mode)
{
    analog_reference = mode;
}
```

The `analogRead()` function is a bit more interesting (actually, 10 bits more interesting). From the preceding chapter we saw that there several registers associated with the ADC system. For single conversion operation the important registers include `ADCSRA` (ADC control and status register A) and `ADMUX` (ADC multiplexer selection register). The register bits are repeated below for convenience:

Register	Bit 7	Bit 6	Bit 5	Bit 4	Bit 3	Bit 2	Bit 1	Bit 0
ADCSRA	ADEN	ADSC	ADATE	ADIF	ADIE	ADPS2	ADPS1	ADPS0
ADMUX	REFS1	REFS0	ADLAR	-	MUX3	MUX2	MUX1	MUX0

Figure 26.2, ADC bits

Also recall that the `ADCH` and `ADCL` registers contain the high and low bytes of the result, respectively. For `ADCSRA`, setting `ADEN` enables the ADC. Setting `ADSC` starts a conversion. It will stay at one until the conversion is complete, the hardware resetting it to zero. `ADIF` and `ADIE` are used with an interrupt-based mode not discussed here. `ADATE` stands for AD Auto Trigger Enable which allows triggering of the ADC from an external signal (again, not discussed here). `ADPSx` are pre-scaler bits which set the conversion speed. See the previous chapter for details.

For `ADMUX`, `REFSx` sets the reference voltage source where 00 = use `AREF` pin, 01 = use `VCC`, 10 = reserved, 11 = use internal 1.1 volt reference. Setting `ADLAR` left-adjusts the 10 bit word within the `ADCH` and `ADCL` result registers (i.e. it left-justifies, leaving the bottom six bits unused). Clearing this bit leaves the result right justified (i.e. top six bits are unused). The four `MUXx` bits select which input channel is used for the conversion. For example, to read from channel 5, set these bits to the pattern 0101.

Other registers are available such as `ADSRB` and `ACSR` which are useful for other modes of operation. They are not necessary for the current purpose, though.

The code follows, cleaned up for ease of reading. The original code contains a considerable number of `#ifdefs` so it works with different microcontrollers.

```c
int analogRead(uint8_t pin)
{
    uint8_t low, high;

    if (pin >= 14) pin -= 14; // allow for channel or pin numbers

    // set the analog reference, input pin and clear left-justify (ADLAR)
    ADMUX = (analog_reference << 6) | (pin & 0x07);

    // start the conversion
    sbi(ADCSRA, ADSC);

    // ADSC is cleared when the conversion finishes
    while (bit_is_set(ADCSRA, ADSC));

    // read low and high bytes of result
    low  = ADCL;
    high = ADCH;

    // combine the two bytes
    return (high << 8) | low;
}
```

Figure 26.3, analogRead code

Embedded Controllers

Let's take a closer look. First, two unsigned bytes are declared to hold the contents of the high and low result registers; then the pin argument is translated. Note the undocumented usage of either channel or pin numbers. Always be cautious about using undocumented features.

```
uint8_t low, high;

if (pin >= 14) pin -= 14; // allow for channel or pin numbers
```

At this point the reference is set (note how the `analog_reference` global is shifted up to the `REFSx` bits). The `pin` number is ANDed with 0x07 for safety and ORed into `ADMUX`. Note that the result will be right-justified as `ADLAR` is not set.

```
ADMUX = (analog_reference << 6) | (pin & 0x07);
```

The conversion is initiated by setting the AD Start Conversion bit. `sbi()` is a macro that reduces to a single "set bit" instruction in assembly. We then wait until the `ADSC` bit is cleared which signifies the conversion is complete. The `while` loop is referred to properly as a "busy-wait" loop; the code simply "sits" on that bit, checking it over and over until it is finally cleared. This causes the loop to exit. Again, `bit_is_set()` is a macro that returns `true` if the bit under test is set to one and `false` if it's clear.

```
// start the conversion
sbi(ADCSRA, ADSC);

// ADSC is cleared when the conversion finishes
while ( bit_is_set(ADCSRA, ADSC) );
```

The conversion is now complete. `ADCL` must be read first as doing so locks both the `ADCL` and `ADCH` registers until `ADCH` is read. Doing the reverse could result in spurious values. The two bytes are then combined into a single 16 bit integer result by ORing the low byte with the left-shifted high byte. As the data in the result registers were right-justified, the top six bits will be zeros in the returned integer, resulting in an output range of 0 through 1023.

```
low  = ADCL;
high = ADCH;

// combine the two bytes
return (high << 8) | low;
```

Given the default prescaler values and function call overhead, the maximum conversion rate is approximately 10 kHz which is perfectly acceptable for a wide variety of uses. The function is fairly bare-bones and straightforward to use as is. Use this function as a guide if you wish to produce left-justified data (set `ADLAR` bit) or other simple modifications. If time is of the essence and machine cycles cannot be wasted with the busy-wait loop seen above, an interrupt-based version or free-running version may be a better choice.

26.2 A Practical Example: Mapping a Sensor

As mentioned at the outset, the analog input system may be used to obtain data from a variety of sensors. One potential issue is that the range of sensor output voltages may not conveniently "line up" with the ADC input range, thus requiring some form of data scaling and offsetting. That is, the input voltages will need to be mapped onto a range of desired numeric output values. Sometimes this can be done with hardware but other times a simple mathematical process will suffice.

For example, suppose we have a sensor that we'll use for measuring the temperature of liquid water at standard pressure. The specifications indicate that the unit will produce one volt at freezing (32 degrees Fahrenheit) and three volts at boiling (212 degrees Fahrenheit). Assuming that we're using the default reference which yields an input range of zero to five volts, we'll only be using 40% of the available dynamic range (i.e., two volts out of five). To make full use of the ten bit ADC, we'd need to run the sensor through a signal conditioning circuit to map the two volt output range onto the five volt input range. This would require an amplifier with a level shift of one volt and a voltage gain of 2.5. That is, we subtract one volt from the sensor output and then multiply the result by 2.5. By doing so, the 32 degree output of one volt will produce zero volts and the 212 degree output of three volts will produce five volts. A modest op amp or discrete transistor stage can be designed to achieve this. At the ADC input the total range of 180 degrees will be divided up into 1024 levels, yielding a resolution of better than 0.2 degrees per step. Note that the numeric values from the ADC are not the temperature values. A temperature of 32 degrees yields an ADC output of zero while 212 degrees produces 1023 from the ADC. If we need to display the Fahrenheit temperatures, perhaps on a multiplexed seven segment or LCD display, we'll need to map these. This can be done with a simple formula that we'll look at in a moment or with the Arduino `map()` function.

If a more modest resolution can be tolerated, a simple software mapping can be used. If we take the sensor output "as is", we have to accept that we'll only be getting 40% of the available resolution in this example. That will still give us around one-half degree resolution. Assuming this is sufficient, for the numeric readout just mentioned, all we need to do is map an input voltage of one volt to a numeric output of 32 and an input of three volts to a numeric output of 212. The one volt input represents one-fifth of the ADC's maximum input signal and would produce a value of approximately 205. The three volt input would produce approximately 614. 205 represents the offset of 32 degrees and the range of 614−205 or 409 needs to represent the temperature range of 180 degrees. We can do this with one small formula:

```
// av is the value returned from analogRead() and
// dv is the value to be displayed

dv = 32+180*(av-205)/409;
```

Note that this computation is done entirely with integer math rather than floating point for best possible speed and minimal compiled code. For very large values of the variable `av` the product could overflow an `unsigned int` so a `long` computation would be needed. Note that the multiply must be done before the integer divide or a horrendous loss of precision will occur due to truncation. `dv` itself could still be a `short` (or even an `unsigned char`), so a little creative casting might yield something like this:

```
dv = (short)(32+180*(long)(av-205)/409);
```

As we are using integers, the displayed temperature resolution will be one degree (truncating).

26.3 Exercise

Using a sensor that produces two volts at freezing and four volts at boiling, describe a circuit that will scale the sensor output to a zero-to-five volt input range along with the code required to display the associated values in Celsius (i.e., two volts displays 0 and four volts displays 100).

27. Bits & Pieces: analogWrite()

While some more advanced microcontrollers contain a digital to analog converter (DAC) to produce a continuously variable analog output signal, most do not. The ATmega 328P on the Uno is one of those that don't. How then can we get the controller to produce analog signals? One method is to use an entire bank of port pins, say all eight bits of port B, and feed these directly to an external parallel-input DAC. We then write each byte to the port at the desired rate. The DAC (along with a low-pass reconstruction filter) reconstructs these data into a smooth signal. The second method relies on pulse width modulation. This scheme is employed on the Uno and many other Arduino boards. Note that not all loads will operate properly with a simple PWM signal. Some loads may require further processing of the PWM signal (such as filtering).

The key to understanding pulse width modulation is to consider the "area under the curve". Suppose we have a one volt pulse signal that lasts for a period of five seconds, goes low for five seconds and then repeats. The same area would be achieved by a five volt pulse that stayed high for just one second out of ten. That is, the average value of either pulse over the course of ten seconds is one half volt. Similarly, if that five volt pulse stayed high for two seconds, then over the course of the ten second period the average value would be one volt. In other words; the greater the duty cycle, the higher the average voltage level. If we sped this up and the pulses were milliseconds or microseconds in width and repeated over and over, we could low pass filter the pulse train and achieve smoothly varying results. For some loads, we wouldn't even have to filter the result. Examples would include driving a resistive heating element to control temperature or driving an LED to control brightness.

The Uno achieves PWM through the use of its three internal counters. Each of these has an A and B component, so it's possible to generate six PWM signals. The Arduino system pre-configures these for you. You can tell which pins are PWM-capable just by looking at the board. PWM pins will have a tilde (~) next to their Arduino pin number. The `analogWrite()` function takes a great deal of work off your shoulders. Here is the on-line documentation repeated for your convenience:

---

analogWrite()[24]

Description

Writes an analog value (PWM wave) to a pin. Can be used to light a LED at varying brightnesses or drive a motor at various speeds. After a call to **analogWrite()**, the pin will generate a steady square wave of the specified duty cycle until the next call to **analogWrite()** (or a call to **digitalRead()** or **digitalWrite()** on the same pin). The frequency of the PWM signal is approximately 490 Hz.

On most Arduino boards (those with the ATmega168 or ATmega328), this function works on pins 3, 5, 6, 9, 10, and 11. On the Arduino Mega, it works on pins 2 through 13. Older Arduino boards with an ATmega8 only support analogWrite() on pins 9, 10, and 11.

The Arduino Due supports analogWrite() on pins 2 through 13, plus pins DAC0 and DAC1. Unlike the PWM pins, DAC0 and DAC1 are Digital to Analog converters, and act as true analog outputs.

You do not need to call pinMode() to set the pin as an output before calling analogWrite().

---

[24] http://arduino.cc/en/Reference/AnalogWrite

The *analogWrite* function has nothing to do with the analog pins or the *analogRead* function.

Syntax

analogWrite(pin, value)

Parameters

pin: the pin to write to.

value: the duty cycle: between 0 (always off) and 255 (always on).

Returns

nothing

Notes and Known Issues

The PWM outputs generated on pins 5 and 6 will have higher-than-expected duty cycles. This is because of interactions with the millis() and delay() functions, which share the same internal timer used to generate those PWM outputs. This will be noticed mostly on low duty-cycle settings (e.g 0 - 10) and may result in a value of 0 not fully turning off the output on pins 5 and 6.

See also

- analogRead()
- analogWriteResolution()
- Tutorial: PWM

Figure 27.1, analogWrite docs

The bottom line is that you call analogWrite() with just the pin of interest and a duty cycle value that ranges from 0 (off) to 255 (fully on). That's all there is to it. But why is the range 0 to 255 instead of the more obvious 0 to 100 percent? Let's take a look at the code, as usual slightly cleaned up for your convenience (the original code may be found in the file wiring_analog.c):

```
void analogWrite(uint8_t pin, int val)
{
    pinMode(pin, OUTPUT);

    if (val == 0)
    {
        digitalWrite(pin, LOW);
    }
    else
    {
        if (val == 255)
        {
            digitalWrite(pin, HIGH);
        }
        else
        {
```

Embedded Controllers

```
                    switch( digitalPinToTimer(pin) )
                    {
                    case TIMER0A:
                            // connect pwm to pin on timer 0, channel A
                            sbi(TCCR0A, COM0A1);
                            OCR0A = val; // set pwm duty
                            break;

                    case TIMER0B:
                            // connect pwm to pin on timer 0, channel B
                            sbi(TCCR0A, COM0B1);
                            OCR0B = val; // set pwm duty
                            break;

                    // and so on for TIMER1A through TIMER2B

                    case NOT_ON_TIMER:
                    default:
                            if (val < 128)
                                    digitalWrite(pin, LOW);
                            else
                                    digitalWrite(pin, HIGH);
                    }
                }
        }
}
```

Figure 27.2, analogWrite code

The first thing we see is a call to `pinMode()` to guarantee that the pin is set up for output. While it's possible to simply require programmers to make this function call themselves before each usage, it is safer to place it inside the function. Note that if you were only using this pin in this mode, you could make this call yourself just once as part of your setup routine and make your own version of `analogWrite()` having removed this part (and perhaps some other sections) to shave the execution time.

```
        pinMode(pin, OUTPUT);
```

The code then does a quick check to see if we want fully on or fully off, in which case it dispenses with the timer and just calls `digitalWrite()`.

```
        if (val == 0)
        {
                digitalWrite(pin, LOW);
        }
        else
        {
```

```
if (val == 255)
{
        digitalWrite(pin, HIGH);
}
```

At this point, a value from 1 to 254 must have been entered. The pin is translated to a timer and, through a `switch/case` statement, the appropriate timer's control register is activated and the duty cycle value is loaded into the associated count register. These timers are eight bit units. Therefore they can hold values between 0 and 255. This is why the "duty cycle" value runs from 0 to 255 instead of 0 to 100 percent. (Technically, timer one is a 16 bit unit but is used here with eight.)

```
switch( digitalPinToTimer(pin) )
{
        case TIMER0A:
                // connect pwm to pin on timer 0, channel A
                sbi(TCCR0A, COM0A1);
                OCR0A = val; // set pwm duty
                break;

        case TIMER0B:
                // connect pwm to pin on timer 0, channel B
                sbi(TCCR0A, COM0B1);
                OCR0B = val; // set pwm duty
                break;

        // and so on for TIMER1A through TIMER2B
```

Finally, if `analogWrite()` is used on a pin that is not configured with a timer, the function does the best it can, namely calling `digitalWrite()`. Any value below half (128) will produce a low and any value at half or above will produce a high:

```
        case NOT_ON_TIMER:
        default:
                if (val < 128)
                        digitalWrite(pin, LOW);
                else
                        digitalWrite(pin, HIGH);
```

It is worth repeating that on Arduino boards that contain an internal DAC such as the Due, this function will produce true analog output signals (the code for that is not shown).

Embedded Controllers

28. Bits & Pieces: Timer/Counters

28.1 Introduction

Virtually all microcontrollers contain one or more hardware timer/counter function blocks. These can be used for a variety of functions including generating time delays, counting input events, generating simple pulse or PWM waveforms, and triggering software interrupts. In general, there are multiple ways to configure these blocks. Often, they are set up as simple up counters that are clocked by the system clock. In some instances they may be run asynchronously from an external clock source.

The ATmega 328P contains three of these blocks: two eight bit units named TC0 and TC2 (Timer Counter 0 and 2), and one 16 bit unit, TC1. A functional block diagram of an eight bit unit is shown in Figure 28.1. The 16 bit unit is similar but offers extended abilities.

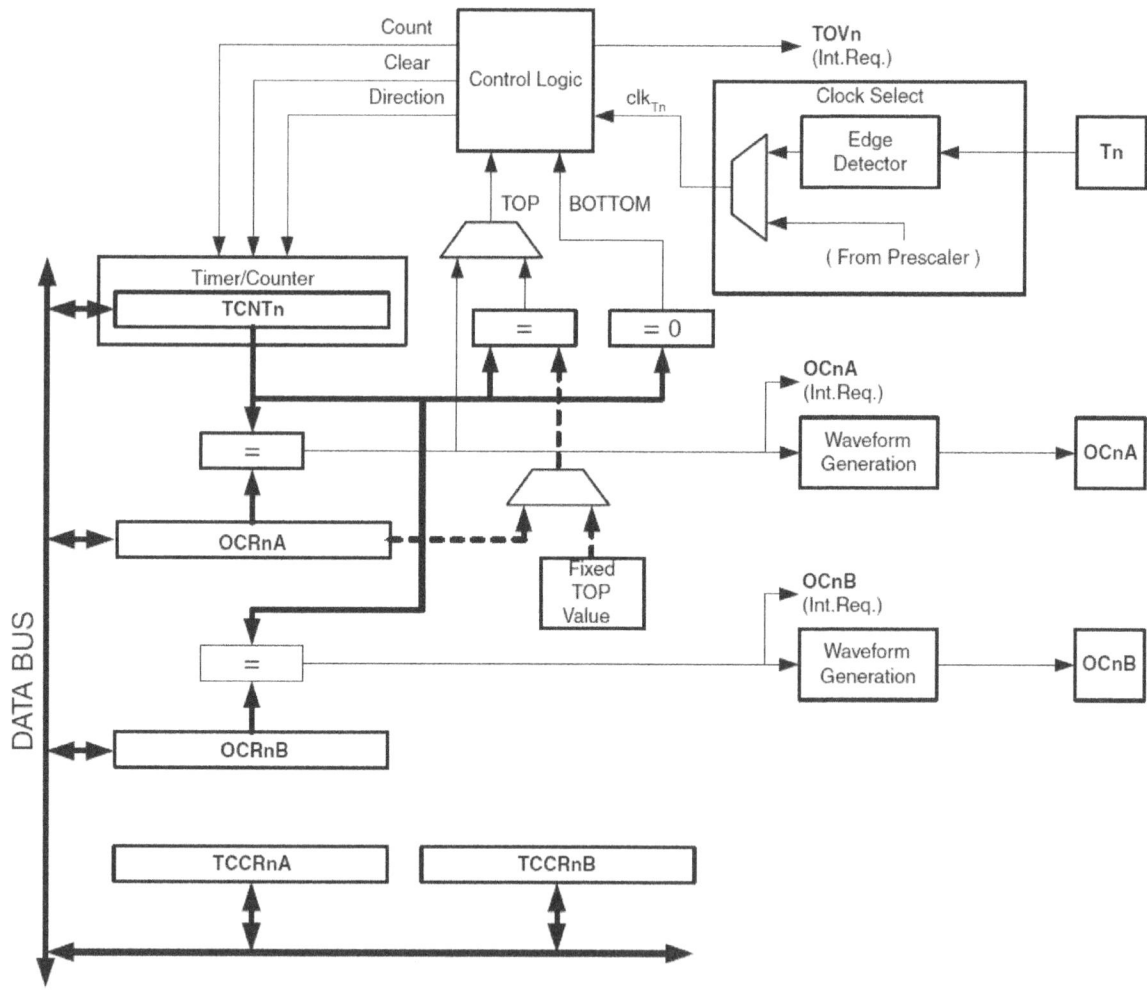

Figure 28.1, timer/counter functional block diagram (eight bit)

First, there are a couple of registers used to program the operation of the block. These are TCCRnA and TCCRnB (Timer Counter Control Registers A and B) where *n* is the timer/counter number (0, 1 or 2 here, although other microcontrollers in the series may have more). These bits are usually "set and forget", that is, they are set/cleared for a given use and not touched again unless the unit needs to be reprogrammed for a different use. More detail on these will be presented momentarily. There are also two registers that are used with software interrupts, TIFRn and TIMSKn (Timer Interrupt Flag Register and Timer Interrupt MaSK register) that aren't shown here. We will examine these in the section on software interrupts. The other key registers are TCNTx (Timer CouNT) along with OCRnA and OCRnB (Output Compare Registers A and B).

In its most basic operation the unit increments the TCNTn register with each tick of the system clock. Eventually, this register will reach its maximum value and overflow, resulting in zero, effectively resetting the register and the count continues up from there. This maximum value is 255 for an eight bit unit (i.e., 11111111 binary) and 65535 for a 16 bit unit. Optionally, the unit may be programmed to inspect the values contained in the OCRn registers and compare them to the current contents of TCNTn to see if they match. Both the overflow and the compare match can be used trigger some action, e.g., a waveform level change or software interrupt. The compare match section feeds a pulse waveform generator that in turn feeds an output pin. This section is shown in Figure 28.2.

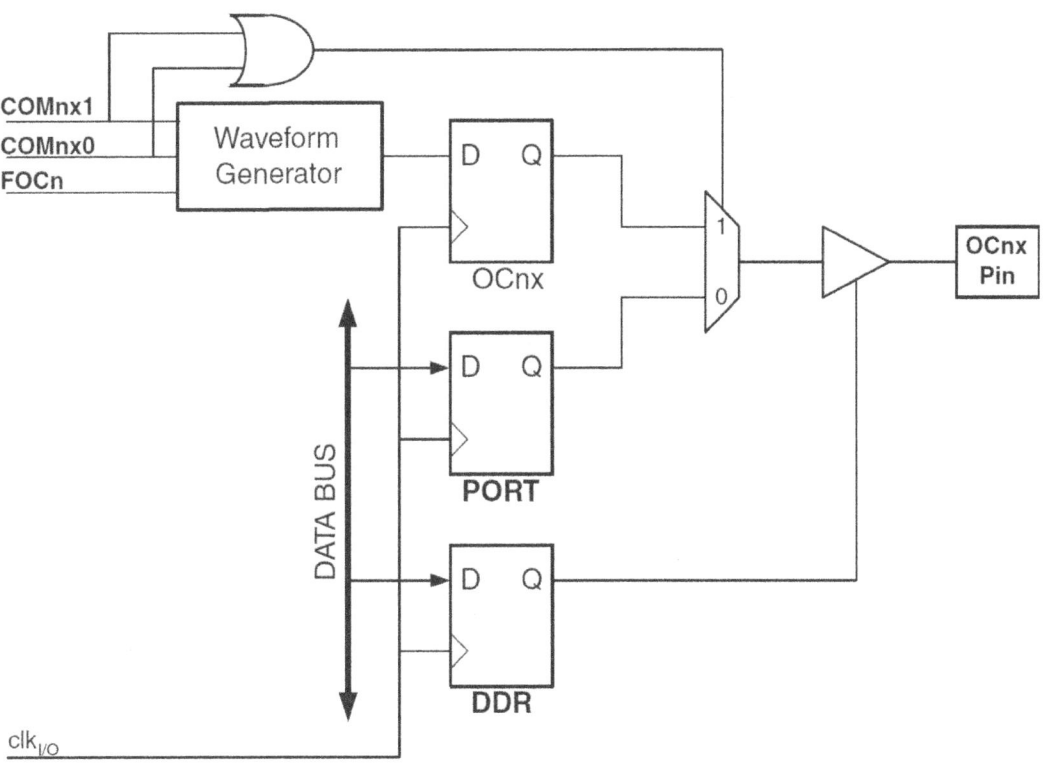

Figure 28.2, timer/counter compare match output circuitry

Embedded Controllers

The box marked "OCnx Pin" is a physical pin on the microcontroller. As it would be impractical to have single purpose pins for every function in the microcontroller, the waveform function is mapped onto the general purpose IO pins. Compare this section to the GPIO block diagram discussed in chapter 19. Note the PORT and DDR flip-flops in particular. The waveform generator feeds a flip flop which then feeds a multiplexer along with the PORT flip flop. This signal is then fed to a tri-state buffer controlled by the DDR which leads to the physical output pin. As there are three timer/counters and each has two compare match registers, there are a total of six physical output pins available for waveform generation. The mapping assignments are shown in Figure 28.3.

OCnx	PORT.bit	Arduino Pin
OC0A	D.6	6
OC0B	D.5	5
OC1A	B.1	9
OC1B	B.2	10
OC2A	B.3	11
OC2B	D.3	3

Figure 28.3, waveform pin assignments

The following discussion will focus on timer/counter number two. This is because timer/counter units zero and one are already used for common Arduino system calls such as `delay()`. Reprogramming the timer/counters could alter the operation of those functions and procedures. Timer/counter number two is a little safer to experiment with in that regard although be aware that all three units are used to cover the six PWM capable output pins on the Uno (i.e., via `analogWrite()`).

The two control registers (TCCRnA/B) indicate the mode of operation. The registers are shown in Figures 28.4 and 28.5 for unit number two. The control registers for the other timer/counter units are similar and details may be found in the Appendix.

Bit	7	6	5	4	3	2	1	0
Function	COM2A1	COM2A0	COM2B1	COM2B0	-	-	WGM21	WGM20

Figure 28.4, TCCR2A register (Atmel 2014)

Bit	7	6	5	4	3	2	1	0
Function	FOC2A	FOC2B	-	-	WGM22	CS22	CS21	CS20

Figure 28.5, TCCR2B register (Atmel 2014)

The first items of interest are the cs bits. These are the Clock preScale bits and they allow for longer timer periods by dividing down the system clock before it feeds the counter. For example, if the controller is running at 16 MHz then each clock tick represents 1/16 MHz or 62.5 nanoseconds. Counting up from 0 to 255 would yield a maximum delay of only 62.5 nanoseconds times 256, or 16 microseconds. If the prescaler is set to eight, each tick is stretched by a factor of eight yielding a maximum delay of 128 microseconds in this example. The prescaler settings for TC2 are shown in Figure 28.6.

CS22	CS21	CS20	Divide By
0	0	0	TC Stopped
0	0	1	1 (no prescale)
0	1	0	8
0	1	1	32
1	0	0	64
1	0	1	128
1	1	0	256
1	1	1	1024

Figure 28.6, prescaler settings for TC2

Turning to the Waveform Generation Mode (WGM) bits, there are normal mode, a compare mode (CTC or Clear Timer on Compare) and two forms of pulse width modulation. We will examine Normal and Fast PWM modes here and CTC mode in the chapter covering interrupts. Note that the WGM bits are spread across both control registers rather than residing in a single register. The WGM bits are detailed in Figure 28.7.

WGM22	WGM21	WGM20	Mode
0	0	0	Normal
0	0	1	Phase Correct PWM, Top=0xff
0	1	0	CTC
0	1	1	Fast PWM, Top=0xff
1	0	0	Reserved
1	0	1	Phase Correct PWM, Top=OCRA
1	1	0	Reserved
1	1	1	Fast PWM, Top=OCRA

Figure 28.7, waveform generation mode bits for TC2

Finally let's consider the Compare Output Mode (COM) bits found in TCCR2A. There are two bits for OC2A and two for OC2B, and although the settings are similar they are not identical (for details, see the Atmel

Embedded Controllers

documentation). The settings for `OC2A` are found in Figures 28.8 through 28.10 for three waveform generation modes and describe how the output pin signal responds. Note that in all three of these modes if both `COM` bits are clear then the output pin, `OC2A`, is disconnected from the timer/counter and operates in ordinary IO form. With other settings of the `COM` bits, `OC2A` is controlled by the waveform generator. It is important to note that the associated `DDR` must still be set for output mode in order for the waveform to reach the output pin. Examine the block diagram of Figure 28.2 for verification.

COM2A1	COM2A0	Description
0	0	Normal, OC2A disconnected
0	1	Toggle OC2A on Compare Match
1	0	Clear OC2A on Compare Match
1	1	Set OC2A on Compare Match

Figure 28.8, non-PWM, Compare Output Mode for TC2

COM2A1	COM2A0	Description
0	0	Normal, OC2A disconnected
0	1	WGM22=0: Normal, OC2A disconnected WGM22=1: Toggle OC2A on Compare Match (Reserved operation for OC2B)
1	0	Clear OC2A on Compare Match, Set OC2A on 0x00 (non-inverting mode)
1	1	Set OC2A on Compare Match, Clear OC2A on 0x00 (inverting mode)

Figure 28.9, Fast PWM, Compare Output Mode for TC2

COM2A1	COM2A0	Description
0	0	Normal, OC2A disconnected
0	1	WGM22=0: Normal, OC2A disconnected WGM22=1: Toggle OC2A on Compare Match (Reserved operation for OC2B)
1	0	Clear OC2A on Compare Match when up-counting, Set when down-counting
1	1	Set OC2A on Compare Match when up-counting, Set when down-counting

Figure 28.10, Phase Correct PWM, Compare Output Mode for TC2

28.2 Normal Mode

Normal mode (WGM22:0 are clear) is the simplest mode of operation. The TC simply counts up until it overflows and wraps around back to zero. On overflow, the TOV2 flag (Timer OVerflow) is set in the TIFR2 flag register. More precisely, this bit will be set in the same clock cycle as when the timer/counter register TCNT2 becomes zero. There are no access restrictions on TCNT2. Your code may overwrite the contents of this register at any time in order to alter the counting behavior.

A short code example follows. The program uses TC2 to create a time delay similar to the delay() function. This delay is then used to blink an LED connected to PORTB.0.

```
/* Simple LED blinker using TC2 to create a time delay
   Active high LED connected to PORTB.0 */

#define LEDMASK 0x01
#define COUNTOFFSET 15

void setup()
{
  DDRB |= LEDMASK;

  TCCR2A=0;    // normal mode
  TCCR2B=0x07; // 1024x prescale
}

void mydelay(int x)
{
  while(x)
  {
    TCNT2=COUNTOFFSET;   //count up from here to 255 then overflow
    TIFR2=1<<TOV2;       // clear flag, bit is set on overflow
    while( !(TIFR2&(1<<TOV2)) ); // wait for overflow bit
    x--;
  }
}

void loop()
{
  PORTB |= LEDMASK;
  mydelay(120);
  PORTB &= ~LEDMASK;
  mydelay(30);
}
```

The setup() function sets the direction for the LED driver pin to output, places TC2 into normal mode and sets the clock prescaler to 1024. This means that each count will occur at a rate just slower than 16 kHz given the 16 MHz clock of the Uno. The mydelay() function initializes the counter's main register at a predefined value (COUNTOFFSET). It will count from there to 255 after which point it will overflow and set the TOV2 flag. We ensure that this bit is clear before continuing using the seemingly backward command TIFR2=1<<TOV2; It first appears that this command should set the flag bit but it does indeed clear it (as verified in the Atmel documentation). At this point we busy-wait on this bit waiting for it to be set. In this example it will take 241 counts to overflow or about 15 milliseconds. This

Embedded Controllers

process is then iterated x times to achieve a longer and variable delay. Note that larger values of COUNTOFFSET will yield shorter blink times.

28.3 Fast PWM Mode

This is the "fast" pulse width modulation mode that can drive an output pin directly. Fast PWM is faster than phase correct PWM because fast PWM performs a single slope (i.e., up only) count. Phase correct PWM uses an up-then-down dual slope counting technique. We will not examine phase correct PWM here.

To use fast PWM mode to drive an output pin, first remember to set the corresponding DDR bit to output mode (see Figure 28.3). Following this, the WGM and COM bits need to be set according to Figures 28.7 and 28.9 as well as the desired prescaler CS bits from Figure 28.6. Finally a value for the output compare registers (OCR2A and OCR2B) needs to be set. The value of the OCR2x registers will determine the duty cycles of the resulting pulse waveform. Basically, TCNT2 will count up in the normal fashion, overflowing and recycling as usual. When the contents of TCNT2 match those of an associated output compare register, then the corresponding output pin will change to the appropriate state. The duty cycle is defined by the total count range (256) and the compare register value plus one. An example is seen below.

```
/* Waveform at external pins OC2A and OC2B (PORTB.3/PORTD.3)
   Fast PWM mode, non-inverting */

void setup()
{
  // enable output drivers for OC2A/B!
  DDRB |= 0x08;
  DDRD |= 0x08;

  // the following is done in two steps for clarity
  TCCR2A = (1<<WGM21) | (1<<WGM20);      // specify fast PWM
  TCCR2A|= ((1<<COM2A1) | (1<<COM2B1));  // add in non-inverting output

  TCCR2B = (1<<CS22);                    // prescale by 64x

  OCR2A = 128; // set duty cycles (0 through 255)
  OCR2B = 100;
}
void loop()
{
   // nothing to do here!
}
```

An interesting new twist here is that there is nothing in the main loop() function! Once the timer/counter is set up it runs without further attention, truly "set and forget" operation. In this case, the output frequency will be the main clock of 16 MHz divided by the 64x prescaler and then divided by the total count of 256. This yields approximately 977 Hz. The duty cycle for output A is (128+1)/256 or about 50.4%. For output B the result is (100+1)/256 or approximately 39.5%.

The preceding code was downloaded to an Arduino Uno and an oscilloscope was attached to the two output pins. The resulting waveforms are shown in Figure 28.11. Note the relative accuracy of the timing computations compared to those measured by the oscilloscope.

It is worthwhile to note that the values of the output compare registers could be changed programmatically, for example via a potentiometer connected to an analog input pin. This would effectively recreate an alternate form of the `analogWrite()` function.

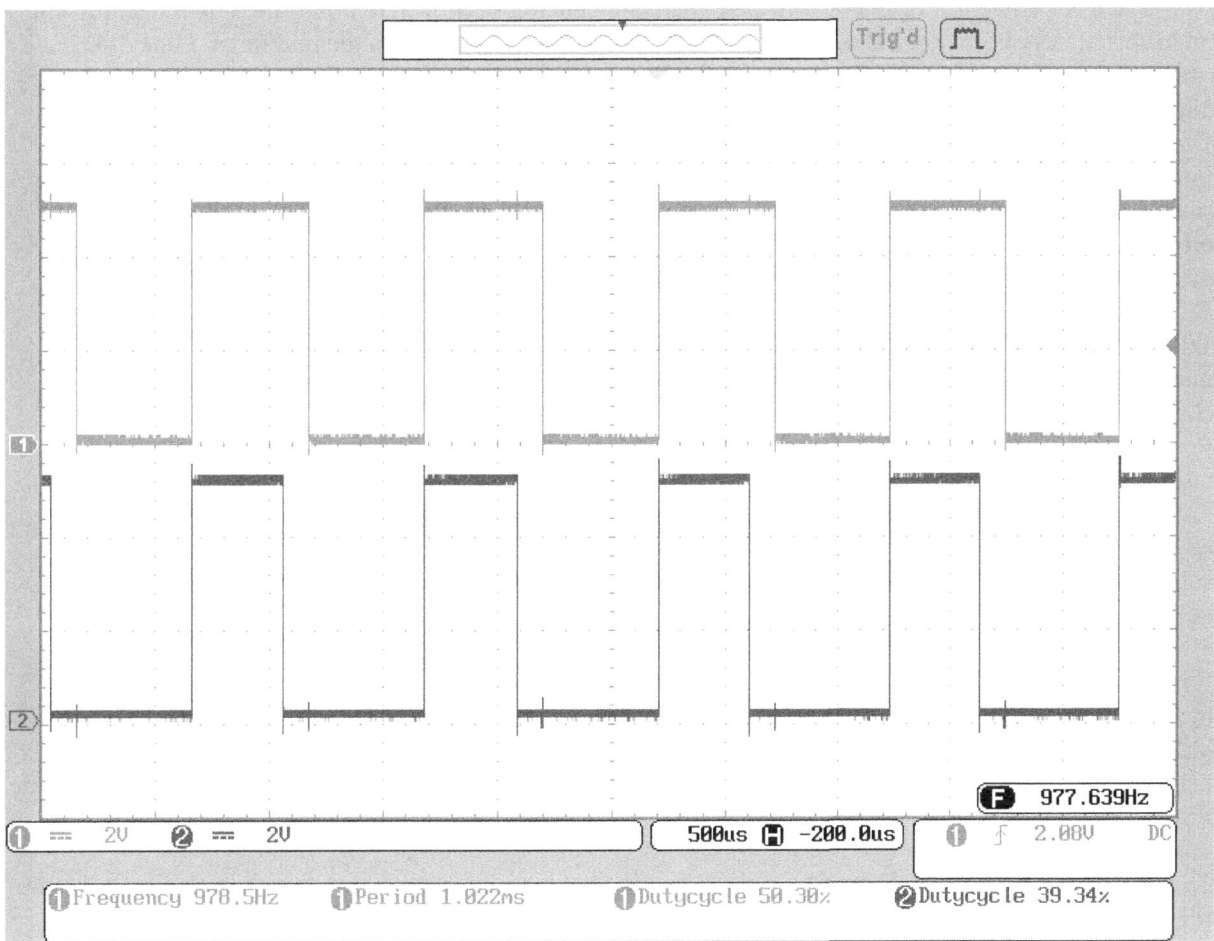

Figure 28.11, Fast PWM output waveforms

29. Bits & Pieces: Interrupts

29.1 Introduction

Interrupts may be thought of as small snippets of code that are of such high priority that the main program flow is momentarily halted so that the interrupt code can be run. Once the interrupt code (referred to as an *interrupt service routine*, or ISR) is finished, the main code picks up where it left off. When dealing with interrupts always keep in mind that they could happen at any time, even in the middle of a line of C code (this is due to the fact that a single line of C might generate several lines of native machine code and the interrupt could occur in between machine code instructions).

Interrupts usually come from two sources: an externally triggered event such as a physical pin changing state or via an internally triggered event. For example, an external switch could be used to force the program to reset itself from the start. Alternately, the overflow and compare match events of internal timer/counters are often used to create internal interrupts that can control the timing of other events.

When an interrupt occurs, the current state and location in the executing code is saved. The microcontroller then jumps to the starting address of the ISR. The ISR code is executed and upon completion program flow reverts back to where it left off in the main sequence. As the main program flow is being halted temporarily, ISRs are designed to be short and to execute quickly so as to have minimal timing impact on the main code. As most microcontrollers have numerous sources for interrupts, interrupts are usually prioritized, some being more important than others. This means it is possible for one interrupt to interrupt another interrupt (i.e., nested interrupts having different priorities). In this way, something like a fire alarm sensor could take precedence over a more mundane sensor input such as a volume control.

It is quite possible for a complicated application to have over a dozen possible interrupt sources. Each of these will have its own ISR. The starting locations of the ISRs are found in a *vector table*. A vector table is basically an array of pointers. In this case, these pointers point to the starting address of some code rather than to the addresses of variables. Some programmers will use the word "vector" as a verb as in "the code flow *vectors off* to the ISR".

To simplify programming, the names of the ISRs are predetermined. As a programmer you simply need to fill in the code for the ISR. This might be as simple as setting a global variable. When the program is compiled, the predetermined name is noted in your code and then expanded into the vector table for you automatically. Generally speaking, ISRs do not take arguments nor do you need to create function prototypes for them. A list of ISR names for the ATmega 328P series is shown in Figure 29.1. This list is taken directly from the hardware profile file `include/avr/iom328p.h`. Note that each ISR name ends in _vect while the first portion of the name indicates the hardware with which it associated. A quick scan of the list should reveal a number of hardware elements covered earlier such as the three timer/counters and the analog to digital converter.

Finally, before these interrupts can be used the desired interrupt must be enabled by setting the appropriate bit in the associated register (`EIMSK`, External Interrupt MaSK; `TIMSKx`, Timer Interrupt MaSKx; etc., see the Appendix and following examples for details). Of course, the global interrupt enable must also be set (which can be accomplished via the `sei()` call) although this is already the case in the Arduino system.

```
/* Interrupt Vector 0 is the reset vector. */
#define INT0_vect            _VECTOR(1)    /* External Interrupt Request 0 */
#define INT1_vect            _VECTOR(2)    /* External Interrupt Request 1 */
#define PCINT0_vect          _VECTOR(3)    /* Pin Change Interrupt Request 0 */
#define PCINT1_vect          _VECTOR(4)    /* Pin Change Interrupt Request 1 */
#define PCINT2_vect          _VECTOR(5)    /* Pin Change Interrupt Request 2 */
#define WDT_vect             _VECTOR(6)    /* Watchdog Time-out Interrupt */
#define TIMER2_COMPA_vect    _VECTOR(7)    /* Timer/Counter2 Compare Match A */
#define TIMER2_COMPB_vect    _VECTOR(8)    /* Timer/Counter2 Compare Match B */
#define TIMER2_OVF_vect      _VECTOR(9)    /* Timer/Counter2 Overflow */
#define TIMER1_CAPT_vect     _VECTOR(10)   /* Timer/Counter1 Capture Event */
#define TIMER1_COMPA_vect    _VECTOR(11)   /* Timer/Counter1 Compare Match A */
#define TIMER1_COMPB_vect    _VECTOR(12)   /* Timer/Counter1 Compare Match B */
#define TIMER1_OVF_vect      _VECTOR(13)   /* Timer/Counter1 Overflow */
#define TIMER0_COMPA_vect    _VECTOR(14)   /* Timer/Counter0 Compare Match A */
#define TIMER0_COMPB_vect    _VECTOR(15)   /* Timer/Counter0 Compare Match B */
#define TIMER0_OVF_vect      _VECTOR(16)   /* Timer/Counter0 Overflow */
#define SPI_STC_vect         _VECTOR(17)   /* SPI Serial Transfer Complete */
#define USART_RX_vect        _VECTOR(18)   /* USART, Rx Complete */
#define USART_UDRE_vect      _VECTOR(19)   /* USART, Data Register Empty */
#define USART_TX_vect        _VECTOR(20)   /* USART, Tx Complete */
#define ADC_vect             _VECTOR(21)   /* ADC Conversion Complete */
#define EE_READY_vect        _VECTOR(22)   /* EEPROM Ready */
#define ANALOG_COMP_vect     _VECTOR(23)   /* Analog Comparator */
#define TWI_vect             _VECTOR(24)   /* Two-wire Serial Interface */
#define SPM_READY_vect       _VECTOR(25)   /* Store Program Memory Read */
```

Figure 29.1, ISR vector table names

29.2 External Interrupts

Let's consider an external interrupt first. In this case, the state change seen at an external pin causes an interrupt. We will use External Interrupt Request 0, also known as the INT0 vector. This interrupt examines state changes at PORTD.2, Uno pin 2. Our example will be fairly simple: we attach a passive switch using the internal pull-up to pin 2. When the switch is activated it will toggle an LED connected to Uno pin 8 (PORTB.0). The code follows:

```
/* External Interrupt Example, INT0
   External interrupt pin lights an LED

   Active high LED attached to PORTB.0
   Switch on Uno pin 2, falling edge triggers external pin interrupt 0,
   ISR toggles LED at PORTB.0
*/

#define LEDMASK 0x01

void setup()
{
  DDRB |= LEDMASK;
```

```
    // set Uno pin 2 for input with pull-up
    DDRD &= ~(0x04);
    PORTD |= 0x04;

    EIMSK |= (1<<INT0); // enable external interrupt INT0 (Uno pin 2)
    EICRA |= (1<<ISC01); // trigger INT0 on falling edge
}

ISR(INT0_vect)
{
    PORTB ^= LEDMASK; // toggle LED
}

void loop()
{
}
```

After setting the IO pins, the code sets the INT0 bit in the EIMSK register to enable the interrupt. The External Interrupt Control Register (EICRA) is programmed to trigger on a falling (negative going) edge. When the switch is activated, the falling edge triggers the ISR to run. The ISR simply toggles the bit that the LED is tied to. Note that there is no port setting and pin examination in the main code. In fact, loop() is empty and does nothing.

Among other things, an external interrupt such as this is very useful for high importance items such as a panic switch.

29.3 Internal Interrupts: Blinking LED

In this section we shall examine a series of examples using interrupts trigger by the internal timer/counters. This technique makes use of either the overflow or compare match events. It is usually used when you wish to have events occur at predictable times but without the penalty and limitations of using a simple delay() style approach. That is, the triggers for these events will not need your attention in the main program loop but will generally be of a "set and forget" variety. There is a Timer Interrupt MaSK register for each of the counters (TIMSK0, TIMSK1 and TIMSK2). The appropriate bit(s) must be set to enable the desired interrupt.

The first example shows a simple method of blinking an LED "hands off". The duty cycle of the blink will always be 50% although it is possible to alter this. The example also shows how to generate long time intervals from an eight bit timer/counter through the use of a global variable. The example is shown below.

```
/* Timer/Counter Interrupt Example
   Shows how to blink an LED "hands off" using overflow
   Also shows how to get a large timing value from an 8 bit counter
   normal count mode
*/
volatile int g_time = 0;

#define LEDMASK 0x01
```

```
#define ISR_COUNT 50

void setup()
{
  DDRB |= LEDMASK;

  TCCR2A = 0;    //  normal mode, OC2x pin disconnected
  TCCR2B = 0x07; // 1024x prescale

  TIMSK2 = (1<<TOIE2);  // enable overflow interrupt
}

ISR(TIMER2_OVF_vect)
{
  if(!g_time)
    PORTB ^= LEDMASK;

  g_time++;
  if( g_time >= ISR_COUNT )
    g_time = 0;
}

void loop()
{
}
```

Timer/counter 2 is used here in normal mode meaning that it will count from 0 to 255 and then overflow and repeat. The prescaler is set for 1024x, producing ticks at about 16 kHz. The overflow interrupt for this counter is then enabled. This triggers the `TIMER2_OVF_vect`.

A full count from 0 to 255 will create an overflow at a rate of slightly over 60 Hz. This means that the LED will have a single on/off cycle at a rate of about 30 per second which is a little too fast for the naked eye. Therefore we can't simply toggle the LED as it will always appear on. Instead, we make use of a global variable, `g_time`, that will keep track of how many times the interrupt has occurred. Once it hits our predetermined maximum, `ISR_COUNT`, it will be reset and the LED toggled. We now have a blinking LED that is completely "hands off" as far as the main code flow is concerned. Again, note that `loop()` is empty. This will continue to be the case in the remaining examples.

29.4 Internal Interrupts: Hand Wrought PWM

Our next example shows how a timer/counter overflow can be used to create a PWM signal at an arbitrary pin (i.e., not just at the OCnx pins). For this example we shall forego the use of an LED indicator and simply inspect the signal with an oscilloscope. The output frequency is slightly over 60 Hz and the duty cycle is set by a `#define` although it could just as easily be set by a variable. The duty cycle is `(OVF_COUNT_START+1)/256`. Thus, a value of 128 yields approximately 50% while a value of 50 yields nearly 20%. The output pin is set to Uno pin 8 or PORTB.0. The code follows:

```
/* Timer/Counter Interrupt Example
   Shows how to create hand wrought PWM at an arbitrary pin
*/
```

```
#define ARBPINMASK 0x01
#define OVF_COUNT_START 128

void setup()
{
  DDRB |= ARBPINMASK;

  TCCR2A = 0;    // normal mode, OC2x pin disconnected
  TCCR2B = 0x07; // 1024x prescale

  TIMSK2 = (1<<TOIE2);      // enable overflow interrupt
  TCNT2 = OVF_COUNT_START;  // init counter, count up from here
}

ISR(TIMER2_OVF_vect)
{
  if( PORTB &= ARBPINMASK )
    TCNT2 = OVF_COUNT_START;
  else
    TCNT2 = 255-OVF_COUNT_START;

  PORTB ^= ARBPINMASK;
}

void loop()
{
}
```

The code is very similar to that of the prior example with the addition of the alteration of the TCNT2 count register. Each interrupt causes the pin to toggle, however, unlike the previous example the count register is set to a new starting value which shortens the count time (i.e., the time to overflow). Further, the reset value is dependent on whether the current output level is high or low.

29.5 Internal Interrupts: CTC Mode

This example also involves toggling an arbitrary output pin although the OCnx pin could be piggybacked if desired. Instead of PWM, this example varies the frequency of a square wave using Clear Timer on Compare (CTC) mode. This mode simply counts up to the value stored in the output compare match register (OCR2A) and then resets back to zero.

```
/* Timer/Counter Interrupt Example
   Uses CTC mode (Clear Timer on Compare)
*/

#define ARBPINMASK 0x01
#define COMPARE_MATCH 128

void setup()
{
  DDRB |= ARBPINMASK;
```

```c
    // enable output driver for OC2A for piggyback!
    DDRB |= 0x08;

    TCCR2A = (1<<COM2A0);   // non PWM, OC2A pin toggle on compare match
    TCCR2A |= (1<<WGM21);   // add CTC mode, Top=OCR2A

    TCCR2B = 0x07;          // 1024x prescale

    OCR2A = COMPARE_MATCH;

    TIMSK2 = (1<<OCIE2A); // enable compare match interrupt
}
ISR(TIMER2_COMPA_vect)
{
    PORTB ^= ARBPINMASK;
}
void loop()
{
}
```

Note that a new bit must be set in the timer/counter interrupt mask register, namely OCIE2A (Output Compare Interrupt Enable for unit 2A). The Output Compare Register (OCR2A) is set with a fixed value but again, this could be set by a variable. A COMPARE_MATCH value of 128 yields a square wave frequency of slightly more than 60 Hz. Halving the value to 64 will roughly double the frequency to about 120 Hz.

Appendix A

ATmega 328P Register Map

Derived from the October, 2014 version of the Atmel 328P documentation which may be found at http://www.atmel.com/devices/ATMEGA328P.aspx

Address	Name	Bit 7	Bit 6	Bit 5	Bit 4	Bit 3	Bit 2	Bit 1	Bit 0
0x23	PINB	PINB7	PINB6	PINB5	PINB4	PINB3	PINB2	PINB1	PINB0
0x24	DDRB	DDB7	DDB6	DDB5	DDB4	DDB3	DDB2	DDB1	DDB0
0x25	PORTB	PORTB7	PORTB6	PORTB5	PORTB4	PORTB3	PORTB2	PORTB1	PORTB0
0x26	PINC	-	PINC6	PINC5	PINC4	PINC3	PINC2	PINC1	PINC0
0x27	DDRC	-	DDC6	DDC5	DDC4	DDC3	DDC2	DDC1	DDC0
0x28	PORTC	-	PORTC6	PORTC5	PORTC4	PORTC3	PORTC2	PORTC1	PORTC0
0x29	PIND	PIND7	PIND6	PIND5	PIND4	PIND3	PIND2	PIND1	PIND0
0x2A	DDRD	DDD7	DDD6	DDD5	DDD4	DDD3	DDD2	DDD1	DDD0
0x2B	PORTD	PORT7	PORT6	PORTD5	PORTD4	PORTD3	PORTD2	PORTD1	PORTD0
0x2C–34	Reserved	-	-	-	-	-	-	-	-
0x35	TIFR0	-	-	-	-	-	OCF0B	OCF0A	TOV0
0x36	TIFR1	-	-	ICF1	-	-	OCF1B	OCF1A	TOV1
0x37	TIFR2	-	-	-	-	-	OCF2B	OCF2A	TOV2
0x38–3A	Reserved	-	-	-	-	-	-	-	-
0x3B	PCIFR	-	-	-	-	-	PCIF2	PCIF1	PCIF0
0x3C	EIFR	-	-	-	-	-	-	INT1	INT0
0x3D	EIMSK	-	-	-	-	-	-	INTF1	INTF0
0x3E	GPIOR0		General	Purpose	I/O	Register	0		
0x3F	EECR	-	-	EEPM1	EEPM0	EERIE	EEMPE	EEPE	EERE
0x40	EEDR				EEPROM Data Register				
0x41	EEARL				EEPROM Address Register Low Byte				
0x42	EEARH				EEPROM Address Register High Byte				
0x43	GTCCR	TSM	-	-	-	-	-	PSRASY	PSRSYNC
0x44	TCCR0A	COM0A1	COM0A0	COM0B1	COM0B0	-	-	WGM01	WGM00
0x45	TCCR0B	FOC0A	FOC0B	-	-	WGM02	CS02	CS01	CS00
0x46	TCNT0				Timer/Counter0 (8-bit)				
0x47	OCR0A				Timer/Counter0 Output Compare Register A				
0x48	OCR0B				Timer/Counter0 Output Compare Register B				
0x49	Reserved	-	-	-	-	-	-	-	-
0x4A	GPIOR1				General Purpose I/O Register 1				
0x4B	GPIOR2				General Purpose I/O Register 1				
0x4C	SPCR	SPIE	SPE	DORD	MSTR	CPOL	CPHA	SPR1	SPR0
0x4D	SPSR	SPIF	WCOL	-	-	-	-	-	SPI2X
0x4E	SPDR				SPI Data Register				
0x4F	Reserved	-	-	-	-	-	-	-	-

Address	Name	Bit 7	Bit 6	Bit 5	Bit 4	Bit 3	Bit 2	Bit 1	Bit 0
0x50	ACSR	ACD	ACBG	ACO	ACI	ACIE	ACIC	ACIS1	ACIS0
0x51–52	Reserved	-	-	-	-	-	-	-	-
0x53	SMCR	-	-	-	-	SM2	SM1	SM0	SE
0x54	MCUSR	-	-	-	-	WDRF	BORF	EXTRF	PORF
0x55	MCUCR	-	BODS	BODSE	PUD	-	-	IVCEL	IVCE
0x56	Reserved	-	-	-	-	-	-	-	-
0x57	SPMCSR	SPMIE	RWWSB	SIGRD	RWWSRE	BLBSET	PGWRT	PGERS	SPMEN
0x58–5C	Reserved	-	-	-	-	-	-	-	-
0x5D	SPL	SP7	SP6	SP5	SP4	SP3	SP2	SP1	SP0
0x5E	SPH	-	-	-	-	-	SP10	SP9	SP8
0x5F	SREG	I	T	H	S	V	N	Z	C
0x60	WDTCSR	WDIF	WDIE	WDP3	WDCE	WDE	WDP2	WDP1	WDP0
0x61	CLKPR	CLKPCE	-	-	-	CLKPS3	CLKPS2	CLKPS1	CLKPS0
0x62–63	Reserved	-	-	-	-	-	-	-	-
0x64	PRR	PRTWI	PRTM2	PRTM0	-	PRTM1	PRSPI	PRUSART0	PRADC
0x65	Reserved	-	-	-	-	-	-	-	-
0x66	OSCCAL	Oscillator Calibration Register							
0x67	Reserved	-	-	-	-	-	-	-	-
0x68	PCICR	-	-	-	-	-	PCIE2	PCIE1	PCIE0
0x69	EICRA	-	-	-	-	ISC11	ISC10	ISC01	ISC00
0x6A	Reserved	-	-	-	-	-	-	-	-
0x6B	PCMSK0	PCINT7	PCINT6	PCINT5	PCINT4	PCINT3	PCINT2	PCINT1	PCINT0
0x6C	PCMSK1	-	PCINT14	PCINT13	PCINT12	PCINT11	PCINT10	PCINT9	PCINT8
0x6D	PCMSK2	PCINT23	PCINT22	PCINT21	PCINT20	PCINT19	PCINT18	PCINT17	PCINT16
0x6E	TIMSK0	-	-	-	-	-	OCIE0B	OCIE0A	TOIE0
0x6F	TIMSK1	-	-	ICIE1	-	-	OCIE1B	OCIE1A	TOIE1
0x70	TIMSK2	-	-	-	-	-	OCIE2B	OCIE2A	TOIE2
0x71–77	Reserved	-	-	-	-	-	-	-	-
0x78	ADCL	ADC Data Register Low byte							
0x79	ADCH	ADC Data Register High byte							
0x7A	ADCSRA	ADEN	ADSC	ADATE	ADIF	ADIE	ADPS2	ADPS1	ADPS0
0x7B	ADCSRB	-	ACME	-	-	-	ADPT2	ADPT1	ADPT0
0x7C	ADMUX	REFS1	REFS0	ADLAR	-	MUX3	MUX2	MUX1	MUX0
0x7D	Reserved	-	-	-	-	-	-	-	-
0x7E	DIDR0	-	-	ADC5D	ADC4D	ADC3D	ADC2D	ADC1D	ADC0D
0x7F	DIDR1	-	-	-	-	-	-	AIN1D	AIN0D
0x80	TCCR1A	COM1A1	COM1A0	COM1B1	COM1B0	-	-	WGM11	WGM10
0x81	TCCR1B	ICNC1	ICES1	-	WGM13	WGM12	CS12	CS11	CS10
0x82	TCCR1C	FOC1A	FOC1B	-	-	-	-	-	-
0x83	Reserved	-	-	-	-	-	-	-	-
0x84	TCNT1L	Timer/Counter1 - Counter Register Low Byte							
0x85	TCNT1H	Timer/Counter1 - Counter Register High Byte							
0x86	ICR1L	Timer/Counter1 - Input Capture Register Low Byte							
0x87	ICR1H	Timer/Counter1 - Input Capture Register High Byte							

Address	Name	Bit 7	Bit 6	Bit 5	Bit 4	Bit 3	Bit 2	Bit 1	Bit 0
0x88	OCR1AL	Timer/Counter1 - Output Compare Register A Low Byte							
0x89	OCR1AH	Timer/Counter1 - Output Compare Register A High Byte							
0x8A	OCR1BL	Timer/Counter1 - Output Compare Register B Low Byte							
0x8B	OCR1BH	Timer/Counter1 - Output Compare Register B High Byte							
8C–AF	Reserved	-	-	-	-	-	-	-	-
0xB0	TCCR2A	COM2A1	COM2A0	COM2B1	COM2B0	-	-	WGM21	WGM20
0xB1	TCCR2B	FOC2A	FOC2B	-	-	WGM22	CS22	CS21	CS20
0xB2	TCNT2	Timer/Counter2 (8-bit)							
0xB3	OCR2A	Timer/Counter2 Output Compare Register A							
0xB4	OCR2B	Timer/Counter2 Output Compare Register B							
0xB5	Reserved	-	-	-	-	-	-	-	-
0xB6	ASSR	-	EXCLK	AS2	TCN2UB	OCR2AUB	OCR2BUB	TCR2AUB	TCR2BUB
0xB7	Reserved	-	-	-	-	-	-	-	-
0xB8	TWBR	2-wire Serial Interface Bit Rate Register							
0xB9	TWSR	TWS7	TWS6	TWS5	TWS4	TWS3	-	TWPS1	TWPS0
0xBA	TWAR	TWA6	TWA5	TWA4	TWA3	TWA2	TWA1	TWA0	TWGCE
0xBB	TWDR	2-wire Serial Interface Data Register							
0xBC	TWCR	TWINT	TWEA	TWSTA	TWSTO	TWWC	TWEN	-	TWIE
0xBD	TWAMR	TWAM6	TWAM5	TWAM4	TWAM3	TWAM2	TWAM1	TWAM0	-
0xBE	Reserved	-	-	-	-	-	-	-	-
0xBF	Reserved	-	-	-	-	-	-	-	-
0xC0	UCSR0A	RXC0	TXC0	UDRE0	FE0	DOR0	UPE0	U2X0	MPCM0
0xC1	UCSR0B	RXCIE0	TXCIE0	UDRIE0	RXEN0	TXEN0	UCSZ02	RXB80	TXB80
0xC2	UCSR0C	UMSEL01	UMSEL00	UPM01	UPM00	USBS0	UCSZ01 / UDORD0	UCSZ00 / UCPHA0	UCPOL0
0xC3	Reserved	-	-	-	-	-	-	-	-
0xC4	UBRR0L	USART I/O Data Register							
0xC5	UBBR0H	-	-	-	-	USART Baud Rate Register High			
0xC6	UDR0	USART Baud Rate Register Low							
0xC7–FF	Reserved	-	-	-	-	-	-	-	-

Appendix B

Answers to Selected Problems

Chapter 3
1.
```
/* Ralph Johnson, June 31, 2112 */
// Ralph Johnson, June 31, 2112
```

3.
```
#include <stdio.h>

int main(void)
{
   printf("Ralph Johnson");
}
```

Chapter 4
1.
```
printf("The result is %f volts", output_voltage);
```

3.
```
int x;

x = sizeof(POWER_SUPPLY);
```

5.
```
Y = Y|0x01;
```

7.
```
W = ~W;
```

9. a) 0xf1, b) 0x10, c) 0x0f, d) 0x11

Chapter 7
1.
```
if(X<0)
   printf("negative value");
```

3.
```
// This assumes the variables are integers
if(X>Y)
   printf("%d",X);
else
   printf("%d",Y);
```

5.
```
for(i=0;i<6;i++)
   printf("Error!");
```

7.
```
for(R=100;R<=200;R+=5)
```

Chapter 8
1.
```
float *fptr;
```

3. `c` is an unsigned character, an eight bit (one byte) variable. `p` is a pointer to an unsigned character meaning that it contains the address of a variable which is an unsigned character (such as `c`). `p` could be two, four or eight bytes in size, depending on the operating system.

5. `&` is the "address of" operator. It returns the address of the associated variable. `*` is the dereferencing operator. It returns the value which is at the memory address referenced by the associated variable.

7. This multiplies `b` by the value referenced by `c` (i.e., `c` is a pointer). It may be more clear to show the pointer dereference explicitly:
```
a = b * (*c);
```

Chapter 10
1.
```
// structure definition
struct Quest {
   float X;
   long Y;
   unsigned char Z;
};

// declaration of an instance
struct Quest Grail;
```

Chapter 12
1.
```
char *x;
x = malloc(1000);
```

3.
```
free(x);
free(f);
```

Index

74HC14 127

ADC, 54, 75, 78, 94, 107, 132–140
Arduino home, 4, 8
ARM Coretex, 112
ASCII, 14, 36, 39, 72, 112
auto class variable, 12, 32

Biscotti, 85
Bitwise operators, 27, 29, 41, 92
Boolean, 41, 91
Bus, 12, 80, 100, 104
Byte, 10, 15

C Compiler (free), 8
Cast, 26, 95, 96
char keyword, 11, 14, 15, 32, 36
CISC, 78, 80
const keyword, 30, 33, 110
CTC mode, 158

DAC, 53, 112, 132, 134, 142, 145
DDR (Data Direction Register), 27–29, 92, 100, 104, 104–112
debounce, 127
double (float) keyword, 11, 14, 15, 25, 26, 48, 49, 52
DRAM (Dynamic RAM), 81

EEPROM, 81, 82, 85
extern keyword, 30, 34

Flip-Flop, 81, 100, 104
float keyword, 15, 25, 26, 30

Global declaration, 11, 18, 21, 33, 34
Global Interrupt Enable, 80, 115, 121
GPIO, 78, 98, 99, 102

Harvard architecture, 12, 78, 79, 85, 110
Header files, 19, 20, 28, 34, 39, 43, 57, 64, 90–96
Hex (hexadecimal), 24, 28, 69, 70

Include files, see *Header files*
int keyword (long vs. short), 14, 25, 26
ISR (interrupt service routine), 154–159

LED, 29, 74, 100, 112, 113, 117, 124, 142, 156

Logical (Boolean) operators, 41
`long` keyword, 11, 14, 15, 26
Look-up table, 52–54, 75, 109
LSB (Least Significant Bit), 30, 134

Macro, 29, 73, 122, 129, 127, 140
Marmot, 61, 62
MSB (Most Significant Bit), 30
Mux (multiplex), 78, 99, 100, 106, 132, 134–136, 138

Overflow, 145, 150–152, 156–158

Pin vs. Port, 88, 104
Piranha brothers, 34
Pointer, 32, 38, 48–51, 52, 56–59, 60–62
Potentiometer, 75, 85, 128, 132
`printf()`, 18–20, 24, 25, 34, 46, 47, 57, 58, 61, 69, 70, 72–74
Pull-up resistor, 102, 104, 111, 113, 127
PWM, 114, 117, 142, 143
Python, 5, 8, 9, 14, 15, 17, 21, 24, 26, 36, 37, 42

Range of numeric types, 15
`register` keyword, 32, 48
RISC, 78–80
Round-robin switch, 127

`scanf()`, 24, 25, 37, 48, 68, 72, 74
Schmitt trigger, 127
`short` keyword, 11, 14, 15, 26
`sizeof()`, 25, 48, 65, 66
SRAM (Static RAM), 81, 82, 85
`static` keyword, 30, 32, 34, 36
Status register, 80, 81, 110, 115, 121
String functions, 38, 39

Tri-state buffer, 80, 100, 103

Vector table, 154
`volatile` keyword, 30, 33, 96, 108, 114, 116, 119
Von Neumann architecture, 12, 78

Waveform, 53, 120
Woodchuck, see *Marmot*

Z (high impedance state), see *Tri-state buffer*

Made in the USA
Columbia, SC
14 December 2021

51408902R00091